"I've gone from a single mom, barely able to afford food, to taking a vacation with my kids!"
Even better? I used to feel so afraid to share my voice and felt uncomfortable in my skin.
Now? I'm taking space and speaking up!
I used to be SO stuck in self-doubt and dependent on external validation.
But today? I trust my intuition and create from devotion and flow.

— **Hadas**

"The overwhelm is GONE!"
Before joining Body Talk, I was stuck in 'I don't know, I don't get it...'
Now? I embody leadership, community, and connection.
I'm able to communicate specificity, magnetism, and sensuality.
SO grateful!

— **Samantha**

"Working with my body instead of my mind is REVOLUTIONARY!"
Before Body Talk, I felt so stuck in my head.
So aware of my patterns. So aware of why I was the way I was. So aware of what I needed to change. Yet crippled around taking action, resulting in even more shame, anxiety, and avoidance.
I made some progress, but it didn't feel good in my body. It was exhausting creating in this way, and try as I might? I couldn't seem to break too far away from my normal.
Even when I made massive changes in my external reality, before too long, my internal state would return to the same baseline.
But working with the body instead of the mind?! Has been revolutionary!!
I'd experienced some somatic release prior to this work in the form of yoga, and that was so helpful.
But learning to work with the body on very specific patterns through this methodology is just next level.

— *Ali*

"I no longer feel behind all the time! I'm so FREE and LIGHT in my business... and as a result? Able to be PRESENT with my BF, friends, and clients!

Before these transformations I was carrying the weight of my clients on my back.

I was carrying the weight of needing to be an amazing manifestor.

I was looking at the outcomes to determine if I was doing it right.

My days were filled with a lot of pressure to do and say the right things.

And now? I feel so free. So full of gratitude for the way in which my life and career has played out. I don't think I'm behind anymore. I know now how perfectly everything is working out for me and I get to share that with my clients.

I move through my day able to be present with my bf, present with my friends, present with my clients LOVING it all AND able to want more without it being the thing I need to be successful.

— **Rachel**

"I've gone from $2k months to $45k months using this method!"

I'd spent a year focusing heavily on mindset and the energetics of calling in wealth before I recognized that there was a missing piece: The Body.

I was making consistent $2k months before I stumbled across a free workshop Sheina was hosting. I experienced such a shift just in connecting to my body that deeply, that I immediately joined both Body Talk and Worthy & Wealthy.

In my first month I made $9k. In the next 6 months implementing and working with this method, I made up to $45k months.

— **Angie**

"I used to feel gross & needy selling... but now? I feel CONFIDENT offering my gifts and view sales as DEEP service."

I've gone from feeling scared and unworthy, to capable, powerful, and grounded.

Before finding this modality, I was in extreme scarcity, didn't have clarity on what I wanted to share, and was always in a rush.

I now feel the shift of identity from 'I don't know if I can make it" to "I KNOW I'm capable of bringing this vision into the world and it's a privilege to be the channel for this mission."

— **Lina**

"OH MY GOSH!!! I've collapsed lifetimes of healing work into a few short months!"

Before this work I had some experience with nervous system regulation but always felt something was missing...

I logically understood there was a connection between "feeling safe" and "going all in" but didn't have the tools to implement this understanding.

My body wasn't allowing the big leap I knew I was meant for... until one day I found you on Instagram and immediately felt: "this is it!"

This happened soooo quickly, I am still astonished!

Within 2-3 months, I experienced a freedom to be myself that would take years (maybe lifetimes) to make.

I'm more authentic in my relationships, way less hypervigilant, and am so much less worried about not upsetting / pleasing others.

I feel safe to express myself and have shifted "I want to be loved and accepted" into "I love and accept myself when I express freely who I am" at the body level.

I'm building my business over this, speaking about sensuality, the feminine, and the body... and showing up online unapologetically expressing what I feel is true for me.

Thank you from my heart, Sheina!!! Your movement has truly changed my life!

— Tanja

BODY TALK

THE LANGUAGE OF WEALTH ENCODED IN YOUR BODY

3 Steps to Expand Your Nervous System's Capacity to Receive More — Income, Impact and Fulfillment

SHEINA RASKIN

Take this book to the next level with guided Body Talk practices for just $22!

Yes, $22... insane right?

Here's why.

Reading a book is incredible, but shifting wealth patterns in your nervous system becomes a whole lot easier when you have a library of practices you get to plug into daily.

The Body Talk Method has completely changed my life to:
- Generating half-a-million dollars
- Facilitating on stage to 200 changemakers
- Impacting over 1,000 clients worldwide
- 10x-ing my income two years in a row

Plus, Body Talk has more success stories than the pages of this book. Here are a few of my favorites:
- A single mom taking her kids on vacation and hitting her first $10,000 month
- Making her monthly income in a day while traveling
- Liberating an emotion that had been pushed down for 20 years
- Getting pregnant from womb practices after months of trying
- Growing from $2,000 to $45,000 months as a mom of five

As a book buyer, you get a special opportunity to join Body Talk right now for $22 for the first month, and each chapter will have a guided audio somatic practice that can shift beliefs that live in your body.

I'm so excited for you to have a full-body experience with this book!

Join Body Talk
by scanning here and using the code
book at checkout to get the $22 offer.

To Mummy for teaching me what love feels like

To Tatty for being the embodiment of devotion

To Kfir for believing in me before I knew how to for myself

Contents

Foreword

In a world where everyone says they want to make an impact and create a movement but very few do, Sheina Raskin offers a new masterpiece of work known as "Body Talk" that has gone on to reach the globe, millions of lives, and help women come home to their infinite potential.

In the summer of 2022, I got a message from Sheina asking to join my Mastermind.

At the time, she was making $700 a month. But the way she messaged me was electric. I could feel her power in just a DM on social media.

This was her message: "I'm so excited! I literally pulled off the biggest launch in my business because I know I'm upleveling and I'm committed to investing in the mentors and programs that I desire! It's happening. Pulling the final pieces together and can't wait to be a part of the Mastermind!"

One week later: "YAYYYYY I'M IN!"

She joined the Mastermind even though it was four times what she was making at the time. It didn't make sense. I sold the offer to her because I saw her in her power. If you assume people can't afford your offers before you even sell to them, what you're actually saying is, "I don't believe in you."

Imagine if I hadn't sold to Sheina because I thought she "couldn't afford it" when she was making just $700 a month. Imagine if I thought, "She must not be ready." If you have a body of work that you're developing, how dare you not sell your offers to someone just because you're projecting your own money beliefs onto them.

So when Sheina offers you into her world, take the opportunity, message her with fully electric energy, and say, "YAYYYYY I'M IN!"

Within the first month, she had made back her investment.

Why? Because she is a woman who doesn't dip her toe in the water; she fully immerses herself in a world of creation, impact through the body, and a unique method that will transform your life forever.

She's gone from $700 a month to now $60,000+ cash weeks, launching books that fly off the shelf, speaking on stages, and leading a movement known around the world BECAUSE of the methodologies she teaches you inside of this book.

As you turn the pages of Body Talk, prepare to embark on a journey through that body that will expand your capacity for more than you could ever imagine. I encourage you to immerse yourself in her remarkable work because Body Talk is not just a book; it's an experience that will transform you into a leader who can hold next-level wealth.

Sheina is THE Embodiment Queen.

Congratulations on this remarkable book. Body Talk is making history and is pioneering a new methodology that everyone must experience.

Sincerely,

Bridget James Ling
Freedom Queen

Introduction

My head is pounding, I feel too dizzy to open my eyes, and every muscle in my body is aching.

It's complete darkness in my small Caribbean apartment although it's midday and a bright sunny day outside.

When will this end?

It's the third day of my body feeling like I'm crumbling and I'm terrified something is really wrong with me.

It was like my body was trying to talk to me but speaking a language I didn't understand.

I remember hearing about a book that was probably what I needed right now, so with the brightness setting at the lowest on my phone, I search for the audiobook, *You Can Heal Your Life by Louise Hay.*

I lie in my sweat-ridden bedsheets, press play, and start listening to the author's soothing voice.

A single teardrop leaves my eye. This woman healed her body, her cancer, and various incredible challenges herself — through the wisdom of her body.

I felt a moment of hope surge through my veins.

I knew I wasn't sick. I practice yoga every day, I eat healthy, I swim in the ocean, and dance all the time, but there is definitely something deeper going on.

I manage my way to the living room and pull out a yellow notebook. I Google the index of Louise Hay's book where she lists physical symptoms and the belief systems that create it.

On the left I listed all the pain my body was in these past three days. On the right, I filled in each belief that went with it.

Oh.

Seeing it so clearly on paper was liberating.

My pounding migraine — my pounding inner critic for not being good enough.

My aching lower back — the fear that I was carrying the weight of the world and finances would run out.

My dizziness — the fear of going round and round in circles with no end in sight.

If my body created my beliefs so physically, well, I could just choose any belief and turn that into my 3D reality.

While lying on the couch and having this life-changing aha moment, I made a decision: I would master the language of my body, listen to its whispers, and learn what actions it was asking me to take so that it would never have to reach the point of needing to scream to me.

I got my sorry self-off the couch and made myself something to eat. I went for a walk to the ocean. I came home and finally joined the mastermind I procrastinated on for weeks.

I kissed the laptop screen when I clicked pay to invest, not because this mentor was going to save me, but because I knew this wake-up call was going to change my life by becoming the version of me that can hold massive amounts of fear in my body and turn it into fuel.

Within a month, I 10x'd my income from $700 a month to $7,000. I hosted my first in-person international event, and launched my first group coaching program. I stopped sitting behind my laptop planning, thinking, and getting stuck in my head with endless to-do lists to grow my business.

Instead I became the version that has the capacity to use my emotions and beliefs as portals into courage, generosity, and impact.

I began to bring this somatic full-body expression into the way I market, sell, and coach through using the wisdom of the body and built a half-a-million global movement in two years.

I devoted myself to practicing the art of listening to my body talk every day, and began sharing the process on social media.

With commitment and determination, this evolved into the *Body Talk Method* that is practiced by hundreds daily around the world and a multi six-figure global movement.

I am privileged to have guided hundreds of healers, mentors, and coaches in mastering the language of their bodies' wisdom so that they could generate so much more wealth and impact and create waves of ripple effects for generations to come.

Your nervous system is a reflection of your income.

Every time you listen to your body talk — the frustration, the doubt, the headaches, the sadness — you are accessing a direct pathway towards expanding your capacity to hold and receive so much more income, joy, fulfillment, and success.

Body Talk isn't a book. It's a dictionary that explains your body's unique language.

Use this as an invaluable resource to help you tune into your mastery, your superpower, and your zone of genius.

Body Talk is not for reading; it's for *living and experiencing* in every cell of your body.

This language is your soul speaking through you.

The divine transcends beyond words.

It communicates through **energy, emotion, sensation, and feelings.**

Body Talk is only as powerful as how much you integrate it into your body. Here is how to experience the most transformation out of this book.

In <u>Part One</u> of *Body Talk*, you will get out of your head and into your body. It's easy to get lost in the world of knowledge. Information can leave you in an endless search for answers. That's why we will learn about the practice of embodiment.

Embodiment isn't something you just learn, it's something you deeply experience. Every trigger is there to tell you something. Every emotion, physical symptom, and thought loop is your guide, inviting you to dig deeper. When you integrate somatic liberation practices into your daily life, you delve into the language of your unique body.

In <u>Part Two</u>, you will learn how to give a "microphone" to all the wisdom you will uncover in the first section. This is where you not only become aware of what your body is saying but also allow it to transform into the fullest expression of your most vibrant, unapologetic, and authentic self.

In <u>Part Three</u>, you'll discover how you can train your nervous system to be the receiver of so much wealth. You will train your body to become a steward of so much more on a body level. This is where you will explore core patterns and belief systems that lie beyond the conscious mind.

Making changes in the conscious mind can only take you so far. It's the shifts that happen on the body that really drive transformation.

I'm so excited to embark on this journey with you!

The most powerful way to experience this is by letting yourself experience every page, every emotion, and every sensation as an invitation to feel, move, and integrate into YOUR body!

It's time to go on a wild journey together.

I'll see you inside.

Sheina

Part I: Somatics

Learn The Language of Your Body's Wisdom

What is Somatics?

I am carrying a massive orange backpack containing all my life's belongings. The sun is shining, and I can see my dance team performing to an excited audience on the deck, facing the bluest water I have ever seen.

I'm quite literally fresh off the boat, having traveled over thirty hours to get here.

Am I dreaming? I just landed my dream contract, performing with a dance team at an all-inclusive resort in the Caribbean — but there's one catch.

It's in the Dominican Republic.

And I've never taken a Spanish lesson in my life.

How hard could it be? I think to myself. *I'm sure I'll catch on and figure it out in no time.*

As it turns out, it was way *harder* than I expected.

I struggled to understand what was happening in the team meetings and fumbled the choreography. I could barely make the most simple requests to my teammates and the guests.

But like any language, it's less about grammar and conjugation and more about your willingness to break your teeth.

Discomfort is your biggest teacher. Your capacity to look like a fool, to make mistakes that have kids laughing in your face because you sound so silly, to ask the person for the tenth time to slow down — that's where you learn a language ten times faster than in a classroom with textbooks.

In my six months at the resort, I learned more than a new language and countless choreographies.

I learned the resilience and determination it takes to learn a new language.

This skill has carried me throughout my life. It has allowed me to achieve all the crazy goals and ideas I set for myself.

And that is my invitation to you in this chapter: to explore the discomfort of learning somatics, the language of your body's wisdom, and prepare yourself to meet the most courageous version of yourself.

***

'Somatics' is a popular word these days, but what does it actually mean?

'Somatics' comes from the Ancient Greek word 'soma,' which means 'body.' This term can often be used interchangeably with the word 'embodiment.'

Somatics can be used as a tool for healing, trauma therapy, nervous system regulation, connecting to your soul, and understanding your unique body's wisdom and intuition.

In the context of *Body Talk*, we don't use somatics for healing because there's nothing to fix or change. We use somatics for elevation, transformation, and uncovering the unique superpowers within your body.

Your body doesn't speak English. It speaks through emotions, energy, beliefs, and physical sensations.

Part 1 is divided into three sections:

1. The Emotional Body,

2. The Physical Body, and

3. The Mental Body.

Each section explores a different way in which the body talks to you and to others. This can be felt through how we feel emotionally (joy, sadness, or anger), how we feel physically (a stomach ache or sleepiness), and how we feel mentally (worry or doubt).

In our generation, anxiety and overwhelm are made out to be something that needs to be fixed or calmed down.

In reality, they are an incredible life force trapped in the body, begging for a way to be free. It is the gifted that are given this extreme amount of energy in the body as the tool with which to shake up the world and create global change.

How does this transformation work?

Your emotions live on a spectrum, and when they are trapped in the body, they become symptoms or fears that compound over time.

On the other side of the spectrum lies your unique superpower. This is when the energy of these trapped emotions has the space to move out of the body.

The anxiety turns into excitement.

The doubt transforms into trust.

Overwhelm becomes overflow.

Body Talk is the language with which you can transform the energy in your body from trapped to expressed.

But how exactly do we learn this language?

It begins like any language: with the alphabet, the foundation of it all.

The foundation of the body's language is awareness — specifically, awareness of physical sensation.

To illustrate, let's do a simple exercise together.

Take a breath. Let's perform a quick body scan.

Stretch what needs to be stretched, wiggle your shoulders, and make a circle with your hips.

Exhale.

Now, start at the top of your head. Breathe into your scalp. Notice the hairs on your head.

Is there a tightness here, a chaotic mind with ideas bouncing around?

Get curious about the muscles in your forehead. What is alive here? Focus on the temples. Notice the air going in and out of your nose.

Drop into the mouth. Are your jaws clenched?

What's happening in your throat? Swallow. Is it dry? Scratchy?

Come into the shoulders. Is there any extra weight you're carrying here? Any memories that come up here?

Don't change your posture; just watch, as if you're visiting a museum and observing the exhibits as you pass.

Come into the chest. Is this a familiar sensation? Is your chest caving in, or pushing out? Notice your heart rate — take a moment to listen to it.

Drop down into the stomach. Are you hungry physically, or hungry emotionally for love or attention?

Notice your sacral. Is any passion, drive, or excitement alive here in this moment?

Continue into the womb space. Get curious about where you are on your cycle. What life force is being created at this very moment? Is there any pain here? Constriction?

Come into the hips, the central point for major emotions like guilt and shame. Do your hips feel locked or fluid?

Continue down your thighs. Any fear or numbness? Notice the joints in your knees and ankles. Are they feeling tight or loose?

Land down in your feet. Is there a heaviness, or a feeling of grounding?

Watch your body as though you are a curious visitor. Two minutes — that's all it takes.

You did amazing.

You can return to these ABCs any time you feel like you're getting in your head and ready to drop back into the body.

The rest of Part 1 is for after you have done your *Body Talk* scan and you notice a specific sensation, fear, or feeling that is asking for attention.

1.
Emotional Body

Fear

I'm blindfolded. My friends laugh as we sit on a tram after a long day of school. I have no idea where we are going.

It's my 17th birthday, and they're taking me to a surprise location. They say I can only take off the blindfold when they say so.

They sit me down on a chair. I hear lots of noise and music.

Suddenly, the chair starts moving. I hear my friends squealing in delight and laughing their heads off.

I slowly remove the blindfold.

It takes me a second to register.

I am on an upside-down roller coaster in Luna Park.

Not just any rollercoaster, but the one I'm most afraid of: The Scissors.

Just looking at the ride made me nauseous, and here I am, on my birthday, about to be swung upside down.

I take a deep breath; I was so excited about it being my birthday that I just laughed at the ridiculousness of the situation. Amidst the laughter and excitement, my fear of feeling nauseous turned into adrenaline, and

I actually surprised myself by enjoying the ride.

The nervous system doesn't know the difference between fear and excitement because, physically, they share many features: both have a quickened heart rate, perhaps flushed cheeks, and adrenaline swooping through the stomach.

If my friends hadn't blindfolded me, I would have built up so much fear that by the time I got on the ride, my body would have been too focused on protecting my preconceived fear to enjoy myself.

It takes more energy for your body to fight the fear than to liberate the excitement.

The anticipation is often greater than the fear itself.

When your body has the capacity to fully feel emotions, that energy gets to move through the body and turn into adrenaline and creative flow versus getting pushed down and turning into apprehension and self-doubt.

When you allow your body to feel the fear, when this blocked emotion gets to move in your system, it can finally be channeled into drive.

Fear isn't the enemy; unprocessed fear is.

When you can liberate fear, it actually turns into a messenger. It becomes an indicator that you are close to something incredible.

When fear is stuck in the body, it turns into self-doubt, excuses, and distraction.

Most people try to stop feeling fear and pride themselves in being fearless.

But the truth is, fear doesn't go away. It's not supposed to.

Your body naturally tries to stop this feeling of fear because it doesn't feel pleasurable, but you can train yourself to lean into that sensation.

You can practice by embodying fear in controlled situations and then taking action daily with the fear in your body.

If you want to be doing work that you are excited about, you have to get comfortable with the feeling of fear in your body.

Excitement and fear are very similar body sensations; the only difference is the breath.

The same mechanisms that produce excitement also produce fear, and any fear can be transformed into excitement by breathing fully with it.

If you learn how to breathe when you are experiencing fear, you will start training your body to feel safe with excitement, and that is the first step in doing work that gets you excited.

Your fear doesn't want to be regulated, it wants to be accepted, known, seen, celebrated.

Grief

S unlight is fading through the glass-stained windows of a cottage in the middle of the mountains on a warm November afternoon in the New Jersey countryside.

The room is filled with nineteen of the most special women I have ever met.

I am facilitating a somatic rebirth practice, and although I have only just met these women one day ago, I can see unspoken stories of grief, heartbreak, and loss written on their bodies.

Their postures, their tears, and their bodies are communicating louder and clearer than words could ever.

My capacity to hold the intense emotion, my capacity to be gentle, empowering, loving,

to facilitate so much transformation, was a direct result of my body and nervous system's capacity to witness, hold, and move through my own unbearable pain.

Tragedy is too much pain for the mind to fathom.

So we have to go deeper than the mind:

We go into the body.

When we have the tools to sit with, feel, and surrender to the pain, we can experience the deepest levels of compassion, empathy, hope, resilience, and courage.

Many of us associate pain with suffering, but we only suffer when we resist pain.

Pain is the initial sensation or feeling, while suffering is the mental, emotional, and sometimes even physical struggle caused by our resistance to that pain.

Our initial reaction is to stop ourselves from feeling the pain immediately.

This turns into avoidance, distraction, or physical, pent-up emotion like a knot in the stomach or tightness in the chest that won't go away.

Holding pain is a somatic practice of breathing into the contraction and tightness in the body and creating space for the pain of grief, loss, anger, and sadness to move through your system.

Your ability to hold and process pain is directly linked to your capacity to share understanding, kindness, and hope with those in need.

In times of shock, despair, and loss, the number one priority is not to process and understand our pain.

The first thing we must be able to do is to let the grief in. Otherwise, it turns into an infection rather than a scar.

The body knows how to do this, if we just allow it to.

But many of us push away this pain with distraction, numbing, and avoidance. This is the metaphorical equivalent of putting a dirty Band-Aid on a fresh wound.

It might bring temporary relief, but it has long-lasting and painful ramifications.

The feeling that you are breaking is the preparation for the biggest breakthrough you have ever had.

No amount of inner work takes away fear.

If you want to fully let something go — a fear, a belief, an idea, a past version of yourself — you must experience this letting go in your body.

"I want to let go of fear."

"I want to drop the stuck or the being triggered easily."

"I want to end the dark thoughts and feelings."

These are some of the most common desires my clients come into sessions with, and they are met with an invitation to experience a death ceremony.

Death and rebirth cycles are the power to experience fear in order to have the power to say goodbye, to fully let it go.

Grief in the body can show up as heaviness, tightness in the chest, fatigue, digestive issues, restlessness, or disrupted sleep.

This is often a sign the body is asking you to invite in the emotion of grief.

If you find yourself in a phase of business that feels low or slower, the grief is actually a portal into growth, entering new territory, or an identity shift.

Grief is so painful, and because of that, the body resists fully feeling it because it fears the changes that it will bring.

Grief is the body's way of asking you to let go of a past version of yourself, and that involves your capacity to mourn and let go of something you truly love.

Take a deep breath with me.

How are you?

How are your loved ones?

How are you feeling at this moment?

Let that feeling arise.

Breathe into it.

You are not alone.

What feels like it is time to say goodbye?

Notice how much love and connection you still have to that version of you.

Celebrate her, celebrate the life she gave you.

This new chapter is only possible because of the shoulders you are standing on the past versions of yourself.

Saying goodbye isn't an ending; it's an opening for a new beginning.

Sadness

I look out the airplane window, feeling like I'm in another galaxy. Everything is so tiny, the vibration of the plane from take-off still tingling on my skin.

I look at my father, who is deep inside his prayer book.

I was confused. He didn't seem as excited as me and my siblings, all peeking as much as we could through the window. It was my first time on a plane since I was a baby, and every single detail enthralled me.

"Do you ever get bored of this?" I asked.

"I don't get bored of the wonders God has created; I just experience excitement in different ways."

We land in Honolulu, quite a sight after a long 12-hour flight. A family of 14 traveling across the world. Everyone at the airport stares; it's like a school trip, except we all look the same.

We have to take off our luggage and re-check in for our next flight. We pile countless suitcases on the trolley filled with all our wedding dresses and festive outfits we have packed for our sister's wedding in America!

I watch my father load the suitcases; he doesn't seem stressed about our next flight or burdened by the heavy load.

We are on our next flight, and all my siblings are fast asleep. The jetlag and exhaustion are kicking in, but my father has his reading light and is deep in his prayer book.

Eager to have some alone time with the person I respect the most in the world, I lean in.

"Do you prefer to travel by yourself and only have to worry about your suitcase, or travel with the whole family? Isn't it annoying that we are the last off the plane? It takes so long to go through all our passports, and it's so heavy to carry so many suitcases."

My father looks up with my favorite look in his eyes. This means a story is coming.

> Two men are climbing up a hill carrying rocks in a big sack in their arms.
>
> One of them is so stressed, he is having a terrible time. The rocks are breaking his back, and he is exhausted.
>
> The other man is standing straighter, moving quicker, and makes a couple of rounds of the mountain carrying his heavy sack.
>
> The second man knows that these stones are diamonds, and yes, it is heavy, but he feels so energized and excited about the weight he gets to carry.

"Traveling with my family for a special occasion, yes, it's physically heavy, but it is such a rare and special opportunity. I am so grateful because each suitcase feels like I'm carrying gold."

Heaviness serves a purpose — it's your choice to experience the weight as a burden or as gold.

When I started going deeper in my healing journey, my body couldn't handle the weight of the burdens of the trauma I thought I needed to carry.

I read the book, The Body Keeps the Score by Bessel van der Kolk, and watched countless videos on YouTube about generational trauma in the Jewish community, and started to spiral into despair.

I started getting flashbacks of growing up with a holocaust survivor in my home.

We called her Babushka, which means grandmother in Russian. She was a family friend who stayed at our house because she loved feeling part of a big Jewish family like she had before the war broke out.

Sometimes, we would watch her crying as she would help peel potatoes for Shabbat.

Sometimes, she would wake up in the middle of the night screaming from a nightmare.

I felt such a heavy weight on my shoulders, carrying all of the pain my parents, grandparents, and my lineage had gone through for generations.

That's when I remembered my father's story on the airplane.

I have two choices: allow this weight to bury me alive in sorrow, or use this weight to fuel my mission and create so much change in the world.

I added "Jewish" to my Instagram profile name and began to share more intentionally about the power we carry and the pride of my Jewish heritage and upbringing.

Within a month my audience doubled. The constant neck pain and tight shoulders I was suffering with for months were gone.

Everyone talks about breaking generational pain but forget to mention carrying generational power.

I realized that through sharing stories of my lineage, I get to carry the passed-down strength, faith, and perseverance.

Babushka, this is for you.

This is my promise of keeping your stories alive.

Your body remembers generational hope.

Your bones remember generational resilience.

Your joints remember generational connection and community.

Your cells remember generational intuition and instinctual wisdom.

Your lineage passed down ancestral wisdom that you carry in your body.

Legacy isn't created,

Legacy is continued.

When you go to the core of your generational pain, you can turn it into fuel for change, for impact.

Feel yourself sitting in your seat beneath you.

Bring your mother, father, grandparent, or a special person into your space.

Take a breath in.

Notice any shifts in your body as this character is present in the practice.

Notice the weight they carry, the burden, the stories, the hardships.

Watch them pass it to you.

Reach out your hands.

Place it in your lap.

Breathe into the space between your hands.

You get to put this weight on your shoulders and continue carrying it.

Or

Take a deeper look.

What does this thing in your hand deeply desire?

What strength are they giving to you?

What do you get to create with it?

Take a moment of awareness in your heart.

Does it feel heavy, sharp, open, or far off?

Worry

The Nervous System girlies aren't going to like this, but worry is actually your body having a conversation with God, and it's praying.

When your body is in a state of panic, the words that live in your mind create all the scenarios you don't want to happen, basically praying for what you don't want.

Why is your body praying for what it doesn't want?

Worry actually gives the body a sense of assurance, a sense of control of the future.

Worrying gives your system a sense of trust by imagining these worst-case scenarios.

Praying does the same.

It acknowledges that what lives in the future is a higher power, and it gets assurance and trust that there is a bigger picture.

Your nervous system doesn't know the difference between worry (asking for things not to happen) and praying (asking for things to happen).

Either way, worry gets a sense of assurance and so does prayer.

So, when you're in a state of worry, remember your body is directly communicating with God.

You just get to choose the script.

Lazy

I hear Kfir laughing in the living room; the hairs on my hand start to rise.

I am knee-deep in writing an important email at 8pm and he has the audacity to watch a show!

I tiptoe into the hallway and catch a glance of him relaxing on the couch; my blood is boiling.

I hate it.

Why can't he just do something productive?

Why is he so lazy?

He notices me watching and immediately sits up; his entire body tenses, and he quickly presses some buttons as if he is also working.

I am taken back to the hours I spent daydreaming in my childhood bedroom surrounded by magazines. As soon as I heard the floorboard creaks of someone coming up the staircase, I immediately pretended I was doing something important.

Twenty years later, I am bringing that guilt into my sacred home and repeating that cycle, associating rest with laziness.

The war against laziness is a war against rest.

I couldn't watch him relax because I wasn't allowing myself to rest.

I couldn't stand the sound of his laugh because I was too busy beating myself up for getting stuck scrolling when I had an important email that got pushed to 8pm.

You're not lazy.

I repeat, YOU ARE NOT LAZY!

You are just scared of feeling the emotions you're running from.

And you have been numbing them through distraction, making excuses, or guilting yourself or your loved ones into overworking.

This scrolling is protecting you from what you are avoiding.

A timer doesn't help; guilting or shaming yourself for being 'lazy' doesn't change this pattern either.

Stuckness is literally stuckness in the body.

You're trapped by emotions, thoughts, or fears.

Avoidance is being stubborn — you can be stubborn about running away from discomfort or stubborn about running towards the full spectrum of feeling.

When you tell me you're so stuck you're unable to move, I'm no longer going to try to change or fix you with more information or self-help.

What you're really asking for is liberation from the cage, from the layers of armor and protection that once kept you safe.

I love that you show up even in the most inconvenient times because those are the times that I need the reminders the most.

I love that you give me hints and clues when I am in robot mode, bringing me back to my core in the most subtle ways.

I love that you are so persistent — proof that I have unlimited access to strength within.

Now I don't see you as a monster. I'm finally listening to what you are actually asking of me.

I know everyone hates you, but they just don't speak your language yet. When they do, they will also be able to transform you into liberation.

Doom scrolling is like a smoke alarm; it's signaling there's a fire starting to burn.

You can either leave the beeping, get a headache, and throw your shoe at the ceiling, or you can find where the smoke is coming from and tend to the impending fire.

Doom scrolling is an indicator that something deeper is going on.

Your body is communicating that it doesn't feel ready to move forward. It's asking you to take a moment to listen and the way you do this is through movement.

This isn't something to fix; it's an opportunity to give yourself what your body is asking for.

Take a moment right now with me and close your eyes.

Feel.

Notice your heart rate, any sensations in your body, and what emotions are active in your system right now.

Take another breath, and notice your posture.

What is the current expression of your body in this pattern?

Small, hunched over, notice where tightness lives in your body.

One more breath inwards.

What is this character so afraid of?

What are they running away from?

You don't change avoidance by intellectualizing it; you liberate it when you take a moment to feel, listen, and notice what it is running away from.

What is your body asking permission for in this moment of avoidance?

"The thing we do to avoid feeling creates the thing we are trying to avoid." — Maya Night

I tried schedules, I tried accountability, I tried productivity masterclasses, I tried bribing myself, I tried punishing myself. I tried different foods. I tried different exercises.

And none of them worked for longer than a week.

Until I stopped trying to put on band-aids and actually worked through what I was running from.

Underneath the fear of laziness is the fear of unfulfillment.

When you feel guilty about wasting time, what your body is doing is protecting yourself from feeling pain.

Guilt acts as a shield protecting you from the actual pain of what you deeply care about.

Feeling guilty about wasting time is your body asking you to get passionate about what actually fulfills you.

Dive deep into why you deeply care about time — what's the bigger vision? Get emotional about that. Get passionate about that bigger vision, that deeper purpose.

Feeling purposeful is an active choice, a constant state of choosing.

Do you choose to harness your energy in repressing the pain through guilt, or do you choose to feel that pain deeply and let it propel you into action?

Instead of letting guilt be a shield, use it as a compass guiding you to a deeper understanding.

Feel that pain, let it propel you into meaningful action, and actively choose a life driven by passion and purpose.

2.
Physical Body

Productive

Feeling energized doesn't come just from a healthy lifestyle.

You work out, eat healthy, meditate, go on nature walks, and even go to therapy, but you still can't seem to feel the full extent of your energy.

I used to feel the same way until my plant spoke to me.

Yes, you heard that right. I'm a plant whisperer now!

One of my favorite plants, a beautiful dracaena, was slowly dying even though I was trying so hard to take care of her.

I kept putting her out in the sun, thinking that was best for her.

But she just kept getting worse and worse until I finally took a moment to listen to her.

I realized that while my dracaena loved sunlight, she couldn't handle being directly in the sun.

I had been scorching my plant, thinking I was doing the right thing for her. And the same thing can happen to us.

We think we're being healthy by doing intense workouts, eating salads and smoothies, 5am club, ice baths, intermittent fasting, and reading self-help books.

But sometimes, all of these "healthy habits" can actually be too intense 'direct sunlight,' especially for women and our bodies.

We're pushing ourselves too hard and burning ourselves out.

We are not designed in the same way as the other plants.

Our female bodies are designed to do business in a feminine embodied way, based on attraction, seduction, magnetism, emotion, and deep connection.

The most powerful way to connect to the feminine in business is through your womb.

Your womb is a REPRODUCTIVE organ.

Productive means to produce.

But your nervous system gets confused between mind productivity and womb productivity because of years of conditioning and old beliefs stored in your body.

The mind is an incredible muscle and its function is to file, to organize, to put everything in the right boxes.

You can feel busy and get dopamine hits from checking boxes, but it is not actually producing anything.

The womb produces, which is real productivity.

It creates life, life force energy, art, magnetism, and masterpieces.

The state of creating is actual productivity.

In your business, when you are functioning from 'mind productivity,' you stay chronically busy.

You easily get stuck behind the computer screen typing up your ideal client avatar for the thousandth time, filling out spreadsheets with analytics and numbers, working on a website, planning, branding, overthinking, overfunctioning — guess what — it's all pretend productivity with sneaky dopamine tricking you into staying the busy worker bee.

The Queen Bee has one job: making babies, producing life force energy, and reproducing, aka creation.

That's it. You are the Queen BEE.

You have one job in your business: to create masterpieces, create experiences, create offers, create a place where others feel a sense of belonging, and create a method that impacts thousands.

That's the simple formula for feminine business.

Peak energy and productivity are CREATION.

It's art, it's storytelling, it's nourishing, it's bold, magnetic, it's brave.

When you're in the state of creation, flow is much more energizing than consistency, being busy ticking boxes and doing all the action.

Constriction

I t's 10pm in a low-lit Mexican doctor's office.

We were on a weekend trip to a nearby small island, supposed to be enjoying a romantic getaway but my stomach is in so much agony.

I hadn't been able to go to the bathroom for days, and I felt like I would explode.

Constipation wasn't new to me; it had been a year of constant agony and trying all different diets and doctors but nothing seemed to work.

I reached out for help to my friend and energy healer, Hanna, who lived on the island. My stomach was clearly unhappy with me and I couldn't fathom why. I was eating so healthy, doing yoga, dancing, and practicing mindfulness every day.

It felt like my body was against me.

She asked me if I was holding onto something that was time to let go of. She explained the stomach holds worry and anxiety, which takes more than celery juice to cleanse.

Control creates a lot of stress, worry and tension in the body through a very physical tightness, constriction, and holding on of muscles. This can turn into aches and discomfort.

It becomes very difficult to be in a state of spontaneity, creativity, and imagination when your body is in a prolonged state of contraction.

Going deeper with my friend Hannah, I realized that I was trying to control my relationship, to control our home, our decisions, and our vacations.

In my business, I was always in a state of being of service, and having hundreds of clients listening to my teachings gave my body a state of power that was confused with control.

I learned that I could receive power by being a leader in my business AND by softening in my relationship.

By giving control a different pathway to express itself, it stopped getting trapped in my stomach and had room to flow into trust, tenderness, and deepening intimacy in my relationship.

Embodiment didn't just eliminate my chronic stomach tension, it allowed me to experience power in my relationship in an entirely new way.

> *Imagine yourself as a detective.*
>
> *Take a deep breath, and with every exhale, imagine you are getting smaller and smaller.*
>
> *Now, when you are the size of your nail, we will go on an adventure inside your body.*
>
> *Start in your temples and jaw — get curious about any tightness here.*
>
> *Move down into your neck and shoulders, and watch for any pinching together, squeezing here.*
>
> *Now bring your awareness into your chest and stomach — what is being held on here?*

How much energy is your body taking to clench, to grip, to hold on tightly?

What does this character want to hold? What is it scared of losing if it lets go?

What is a key phrase that this control wants to express? What does it deeply desire or need in this moment?

How can you make your day centered around creating new ways for this control to express itself, perhaps through a boundary or a difficult conversation being avoided.

Fatigue

"Either you have depression, chronic fatigue, or you are just simply lazy."

WHATTTTTT!

I could see red.

I could feel the blood boiling in my belly.

I was furious.

In high school, I kept falling asleep in class.

Not just a tired post-lunch nap, but fully falling into a deep sleep in one class and waking up and seeing another teacher and an entirely different class in session.

My mother took me to see a top pediatrician, and I felt so excited to figure out why I was always falling asleep.

This very reputable doctor wanted to put me on meds, and I was just 16 years old.

"Why can't anyone SEE me?"

I didn't have the language for what I was feeling or what my body was trying to communicate to me then.

I'm so bored, I wanted to scream, but no adults could understand what I was trying to say. They just saw a lazy, apathetic, bored teenager who could use a quick fix to fit neatly into the system.

But there was one teacher who could see me on a deeper level than my struggles in the classroom.

She took an interest in me, not just as a problem to be fixed, but as a possibility to be created.

She could see what my symptoms were trying to say; she saw pure expression suffocated in my body and encouraged me to join the school's dance team.

The fatigue turned into fire.

Soon after, I became the head of dance for production. I had so much extra energy that I started volunteering with special needs kids after school and leading fundraising events at my school, which gave me an avenue to express myself.

That anger, that fire, that fatigue lit something in me.

I wasn't going to be put on medication to fix a problem I didn't have.

Maybe you're not depressed.

Maybe you're not lazy.

Maybe your soul is tired.

Boredom is your body's way of saying you are ready to live an exciting life, and you're tired of doing too many things that drain you.

Most people see fatigue or burning out as something wrong, a sickness that must be cured.

They tell you to take it slow, to relax, to breathe deep, or to take medication, but it's actually the opposite.

On a somatic level, your body is asking you to see the burning desire within to create something incredible, to make a difference, to be celebrated for being so awesome.

Your nervous system is asking you to expand your capacity to experience YOUR FIRE.

Your body feeling burnt out means the flame is dying down, and your body is begging you — *please add more fuel to the flame of what lights your soul on fire.*

It's more exhausting to be tired and fight the flame than to go turn up the fire on your desires.

Fatigue is your body's way of saying, "Feed the fire within."

So when exhaustion shows its face, greet them with one small thing today that is connected to your BURNING desires, and watch your nervous system open to the fire instead of being crippled by it.

The trajectory of my life changed because I had a mentor who coached to my body and saw fatigue as fire.

The doctor saw a problem to fix.

The teacher saw a massive possibility.

This is exactly what is happening in the coaching industry.

When you coach to the minds of your clients, you see problems to be fixed, struggles to be solved, and symptoms to get rid of which creates at best, short-term change.

But when you coach to the body, to the core, to the belief systems, you see pure possibility and depth, which turns into fuel for long-lasting change.

Coaching to the body involves stopping to listen to the words your clients say and start seeing the words their body is saying, the bigger picture, the core.

Your client's body is speaking to you constantly through their body language, their tone, their posture, their sensations, their emotions.

This is why I developed the Body Talk Method, which has guided hundreds of change makers across the globe to master their nervous system capacity and create so much wealth through their body's wisdom, transform anxious energy into their highest months in business, and take the energy of overwhelm and turn it into overflow in their energy, joy, and fulfillment.

Coaching to the body is a skill, a skill that will scale your business because your clients get radical and rapid transformations when working with you.

When your clients have faster and longer-lasting results, they become walking testimonials for your unique method, and it's the most grounding pathway to rapidly grow your income while having more time to be in nature and present with family.

Solving your clients' problems is easy.

Coaching to your clients' bodies, to possibility, is mastery.

Cramps

I lie curling in the hallway outside my Year 8 classroom, clutching my stomach, crying in pain.

Under my breath I was cursing Eve for eating the forbidden fruit and making us girls and women suffer every month. It was almost a given that we just had to suck it up and suffer for the rest of our lives, and over the years I simply got used to taking pain medication as soon as my cycle arrived to not deal with the pain.

As I began to deepen my relationship with my body, I wanted for the first time to listen to my pain, to hear what she had to say, to take a minute and let her tell me what she needed or wanted from me.

We expect others to treat our bodies with respect, but I don't think we give our bodies enough respect.

I mean, our bodies are always speaking to us and we are so often just shutting it up with another scroll, another to-do list, another snack, or another pill.

Don't get me wrong, I've been taking pain meds almost every month since I was 12.

I celebrate all forms of medicine and am so grateful we live in a world full of options: Western, Eastern, Natural, Plants, Herbs, etc.

Period pain sucks, discomfort sucks, feeling anger, frustration sucks, having a headache — it sucks.

But what if just today, instead of pushing away an uncomfortable pain or symptom in your body, try listening?

It's actually got something really important to say, and so many of us live our lives ignoring the messages that could give us so much peace and clarity.

Here's a quick practice that helps me listen to pain in my body:

> *Take a moment to visualize pain or symptoms as a person knocking on your door. First, it's polite, then they start banging and screaming.*
>
> *Notice what level this is at right now, a gentle knock, someone playing with the lock, or breaking down the door?*
>
> *Come to the door and ask them, "Hey, can I help you?"*

No one likes to be ignored or pushed down — especially not our bodies — they have the best memory.

It's not always easy to listen to our pain and discomfort, and we don't have to like what they say, but we get to listen. Here are some questions to nurse your body in these moments.

> *"What do you want?"*
>
> *"What can I get for you?"*
>
> *"What do you need that could support you?"*

Sometimes, the pain needs immediate relief, and sometimes, it wants to hang around for a conversation.

Remember, this isn't about controlling or fixing, but an opportunity for dialogue.

Anger

No, your anger isn't the problem; it's the freaking key to so much change in the world!

I used to be that kid in class who always found something on the edge of disrespectful to say.

It filled my teenage self with so much power over authority, and honestly, it was worth the detentions and being sent to the principal's office.

There was one teacher who saw this pissed-off energy in me as fuel for powerful words and expressions, and she encouraged me to dance and volunteer as other forms of power and control. This turned into what I have today, a global movement where this fiery energy has an outlet that impacts thousands.

When you are pissed off, there is an insane amount of fierce life-force energy pulsating in your body.

If it's repressed, it turns into control, disrespect, or even deep resentment.

When it's expressed, it turns into creating the change from what it's pissed off about. In my business, the things that piss me off like coaches being stuck in their heads and not having the impact they are here on this earth, fuel me into going to do something about it.

It lights the fire of passion and excitement to launch programs with all my heart and soul.

The next time you feel that fiery surge of anger in your body, don't suppress it. Channel it. Let it be the driving force that propels you towards change and impact.

Passion and purpose are on the other side of pissed-off energy. Let it fuel your journey and create a legacy that shakes the world.

We usually associate anger with aggression but that is only when the emotion is blocked in your body.

Anger is the birthplace of revolutions, of innovations, of massive change.

Anger has a purpose.

To ignite your soul's mission into action, to activate, to be courageous.

If you're angry with the healthcare system for letting you down, you can channel that anger into committing to learning and creating holistic healing for yourself and for your loved ones.

If you're angry with women being paid less than men, you channel that fire into building your own movement and supporting other women's businesses.

If you're angry at the school system, you take a stance on your child's actual needs and prioritize creating a space that they can thrive in.

THE WORLD NEEDS YOUR EMBODIED ANGER!

This is what you're being called to do.

We need your embodied anger to channel into momentum and share your unapologetic truth.

We need your embodied anger and liberation to create change and become so freaking wealthy that you don't need to rely on any BS systems anymore.

We need your embodied anger so that you get to hire the best support and guidance for yourself and your loved ones.

We need to stop hating on anger as the issue and start building the embodied tools to process it rather than push it down.

The most authentic way to sell is to feel angry, and then do something about it.

And I get it, feeling irritated or annoyed is something we try to push away because it's not exactly enjoyable or a 'positive mindset.'

In reality, your frustration, when liberated in your body, has the key to the most activating and authentic selling.

When we make frustration 'wrong,' it turns into silent resentment, which eats away at your life-force energy.

If you want to sell from an embodied space, allow yourself to explore this sensation of anger in your body.

Experience this emotion in a contained space and then ask the frustration how it wants to express itself in your selling today. The magic happens when you fuel all that energy into doing the thing that the frustration is asking you for.

> *What do you profoundly care about that no one can convince you otherwise? What would you rally day and night for? What is something that pisses you off in the industry that you will never be silenced about?*

Create from that place of utter frustration and radically disrupt this pattern today!

Running

I signed up for a marathon a few years ago.

I hate running.

The most I could run was a couple of houses on my street.

But I thought, if I could go dancing on the weekend for hours on end and outlive everyone on the dancefloor, I sure as heck could run a marathon.

Well, I didn't run the marathon in the end.

I danced.

I skipped the whole three hours on Jerusalem cobblestone with the song "Fireball" in my headphones.

It takes more energy and effort for the nervous system to run than to dance.

Many mentors begin their business as if they are running a marathon, ticking all the right things off the to-do list. This tires out the nervous system over time, being so much in the mind driven solely by strategy, logic, and fear.

Your mind is running so fast when your body can barely catch its breath.

It's exhausting for the body to be in this pattern of running, searching, planning — it takes so much energy for the body to always be alert, searching for novelty, ticking box after box.

Or, you could dance your way through, create your own fire, your own source of energy, and embody the version of you that's pumped about the journey, not just the finish line.

Flight

I woke up in a hotel to the sound of workers banging as they were putting up wooden boards to protect the windows.

They tell us a hurricane is coming to the island, and the hotel is closed.

My friend and I, still half asleep and recovering from a wild night out dancing, grab our things, jump on the last ferry, and run away from an oncoming storm so as not to mess up our short Caribbean vacation.

At that point, I had only dreamed of leading a thriving business and being in a loving relationship, but as soon as the gray clouds showed, my nervous system screamed, RUN!

Four years later, another hurricane has just passed on the same island that I now live on and this time, my feet are firmly planted.

I trained my nervous system to dance in the rain, to see the gray clouds, and transform the desire to bail into staying and resilience.

Choosing responsibility over running has allowed me to be in a beautiful marriage and build a half-a-million-dollar movement.

It wasn't always this way. My nervous system used to be so busy, constantly planning my escape route, fantasizing about Plan B because it was so scared that the responsibility of this next level would be too much or too heavy to carry.

The truth is, you can't be in a devoted and loyal relationship when your body is searching for the exit sign.

You have built an incredible community, and you say you're all in, but when your nervous system is running, you are sending messages to your audience that you don't actually want them to join, which is capping the number of clients that can join your programs.

This running can look like:

- Going quiet during a launch because your body is running from the responsibility that facilitating to more powerful clients brings

- Drowning the most incredible content ideas with overthinking and overplanning because your body is running from the fear of being misunderstood by so many people

- Holding back from massively claiming your wins and achievements, because your body is running from fear of being abandoned by the spiritual community who believes massive amounts of wealth is devilish

When you train your nervous system to stay in the long game, you will have hundreds of women begin to pour into your spaces with so much more ease.

Here are the steps:

1.   Acknowledge you are running.

You can point fingers at the conversion rate, the marketing strategy, your mentor, potential clients not keeping their word, or other bigger healers taking all the business...

Or you can point that finger at your own feet and open your eyes to perhaps you running away from commitment or responsibility.

2. How is the running serving you?

Bring this running character into your body; give it the opportunity to run. Let all this fire energy pulse through your feet. Where is it running to? What is it running from? What is the runner so scared of? What does it gain from being in the state of running?

The body is talking; here is where you listen.

3. Give it to yourself.

Your body always gives you your core desire. In order to pattern-disrupt and create new beliefs, you give yourself this core desire in a DIFFERENT way.

For example, if your body receives a sensation of freedom from running away from selling higher-ticket offers because it's scared of responsibility, what is another way you can give yourself the sensation of freedom that holds responsibility?

It could be creating an exciting experience for your community that focuses on serving and being in your zone of genius. The invitation to join your offer is ten times easier for your client's nervous system to invest high ticket when you are a reflection of being 100% committed no matter what.

Either way, your body is going to get freedom. It will get it from running away or from responsibility — you choose.

Pain

I remember the trips to the chiropractor's office as a kid. His practice was based out of a Victorian-style home, and I used to play with the wooden horse swings with my siblings in the waiting area and watch huge orange fish swim around in the backyard pond.

My mom used to take us as kids, and I always hated the click of my back cracking; it was painful and scary, and my child's mind didn't understand that the small moment of discomfort led to sleeping better at night, standing taller, and being more focused in school.

Oftentimes, body pain can feel like the uncomfortable sensation of something clicking into place.

I know that my thoughts, beliefs, and emotions create my reality, but experiencing this click in the body, the core of my being knows it.

This click didn't happen in mindset work; that would be like the chiropractor telling me to think my way into aligning my bones.

It's the actual pain of the cracking that puts the system back in alignment.

Some of us call this a wake-up call, others the dark night of the soul, or identity shifts, uplevel, death, and rebirth.

Many of us strive towards goals, busy with to-do lists, and self-help action plans, but the clicking happens in the discomfort.

The capacity at which your body can feel the fear and take action with it, is the capacity at which you can receive that desire into your actual reality.

Feeling the fear in your body is the fuel to releasing that fear or un-helpful belief.

It's time to stop thinking your way into empowerment and start bringing your body on board.

Don't confuse anxious energy for something that needs to be 'calmed down' or 'fixed.'

Anxiety or fearful energy isn't something to push away; it's fuel you get to channel, to create the courage to make powerful decisions and do something about it.

I don't know who needs to hear this, but striving for alignment is just a pretty mask for self-sabotage.

Alignment means things to be in order, to make sense, to click into place.

When the goal is all about feeling aligned, what is happening is your body trying to keep you safe in a box. Your nervous system is protecting you from the fear of the unknown, from discomfort of growth, from fear of failure.

Waiting for your offer to feel aligned and the timing to feel right is just putting pretty decorations on your excuses to not step into a deeper level of self-worth and impact.

True alignment doesn't happen by waiting until you feel into it.

True alignment happens when your body has the capacity to process chaos and confusion while still committing to messy action.

True alignment happens when you commit to a date, when you promote your offer with self-doubt, when you launch with fear.

Imagine walking into a chiropractor's office and telling them you want to feel into releasing your back pain. What will actually make the change is booking an appointment, lying down in the chair, and breathing through the cracks.

It's not fun, comfortable, or pain-free, but if you rely on feeling into it or waiting for a sense of certainty before taking action, you're creating a recipe for frustration and disappointment.

True alignment happens in the unknown and happens when you take action anyway. It doesn't actually feel fun or enjoyable or clear at all.

It's time to break free from the chains of self-sabotage disguised as waiting to feel aligned.

The real magic is your courage to embrace the chaos and confusion by committing to promote yourself before it all makes sense and fits perfectly together.

You choose or your conditioning will choose for you.

3.
Mental Body

Struggle

I look up at the sky. It's a clear day, and not a cloud is in sight.

"Goodbye."

"It's not your time," I hear.

"I'm too tired," I respond.

I am 16, having a conversation with God while in the middle of drowning being pulled by a strong rip current.

It was 30 degrees, and we had just finished a hike and went to dip our feet in the ocean while still fully dressed. One second I'm standing with my friends from summer camp, laughing.

The next second, my best friend and I are pulled out 100 meters in the rough Australian ocean by a massive current. We try our hardest to swim back towards the shore, not knowing we are fighting a massive current of energy pushing us in the opposite direction.

Within minutes, she is underwater, and I am on my back saying goodbye as we get pulled out further and further.

"Sheina."

What, that didn't sound like God.

I turn and our counselor is holding my best friend and tells me to swim with the current.

My physical body was finished; every muscle screamed in agony. I had no energy or oxygen left to continue fighting.

A deeper force woke up within me. I can stop struggling against the ocean. I get to swim with it.

I start hearing our friends screaming. They are standing in a line holding each other's hands so they can reach us without also getting pulled in.

I make it to the shore. I cough up all the ocean water I have swallowed.

I look up at the sky; everything looks different. I look around me, the ocean, the sand, the trees, my friends.

Everything looks new, with a depth of shade I had never noticed before. An hour ago, the world looked regular. Now, every single thing looks alive.

There is no such thing as struggle.

Struggle just means resistance, fighting against what is.

It's exhausting to continue to fight the tide. When we see it as a powerful force of energy, we get to swim with it.

Struggle means resistance, but when you process and accept the emotion, it's no longer a fight, it's a simple conversation.

Feeling alive isn't feeling happy all the time. Feeling alive is the capacity to feel the spectrum of emotions.

Alive doesn't mean easy, fun, and never uncomfortable or feeling happy all the time.

Alive is your capacity to feel the full range of feelings.

Goosebumps, grief, awe, bliss, anger, joy, guilt, ecstasy, shame, powerful, overwhelmed, focused.

It takes way more energy for the nervous system to be in a fear state than allowing the fear to be your fuel in your business.

It's more exhausting for the body to fear rejection than to fuel rejection into resilience.

Your capacity to feel, listen, and take action from the rejection on a body level allows it to transform into powerful redirection.

When you stop struggling, what becomes possible?

What does the world look like in this lens?

What choices does this version of you make?

What promises does she keep to herself?

What commitments does she stand by?

One decision can completely change your life.

Make that decision today.

Impatience

Everybody wants to do Ayahuasca, but nobody wants to liberate emotions through the cycles, seasons, and the pace of Mother Nature.

Our generation wants quick results, quantum leaps, rapid ascension, massive scaling, and cathartic healing experiences.

The disappointment that comes with thinking there's something wrong with you because it's taking so long isn't fixed with another strategy; it's liberated when you surrender to the pace of nature.

We're so busy figuring out how to grow bigger, heal faster, become richer, and be happier, but we forget to tend to our roots — our bodies.

Bodywork takes patience, emotional mastery takes daily commitment, creating new embodied patterns takes relentless focus.

You can't shock your nervous system into transformation.

If you want to create these massive trees of wealth and wisdom, how long are you committed to the pace it takes to tend to your roots?

It's much easier to want to go bigger and faster, but can your body hold and support this abundance?

If you are calling in massive branches of success, tend massively to the roots that will support this.

Mental Overload

We're mingling at the end of a friend's wedding, reminiscing about the last time we saw each other.

We were both around 10 years old when my family spent a summer in his family's basement in Brooklyn when my sister got married.

I am speaking with my cousin, and we are both so excited to learn how two wild kids ended up in similar fields.

He, a recent graduate as a therapist, and I, deep in the world of somatics.

The music was winding down, everyone was schmoozing, not wanting the night to end, and then my cousin told me something that completely changed my perspective.

He said, "I know it all."

And not in a boastful way; he intimately knows his pain, his traumas, his triggers.

He knows all the different attachment theories, and he is incredibly self-aware.

But at the same time, he feels that he wants to go beyond knowing and shift into BEING.

And that is the power of embodiment, to stop intellectualizing your pain and rather create spaces and practices to feel it in your body so you can process it.

To stop over-analyzing your thought patterns, and embody the thoughts as various characters in your body, let them play their part, and move on.

To stop jumping, striving, and searching, and start trusting your own wisdom and intuition.

I'm just going to say it — this sheer amount of overwhelm is a collective call into embodiment.

We can easily get lost looking for safety in knowledge, books, and certifications, but safety happens in the body, not the mind.

If you feel like you already know, but there is something inside calling for more, it's not asking for more information, it's asking for more being.

My mental health got so much better after I stopped working on myself.

There came a point where I was journaling, seeing a life coach, doing affirmations, waking up before the sun, practicing yoga daily, the whole nine yards, but I was feeling worse than I ever had in my entire life.

I could trace my triggers all the way to childhood. I was hyper-aware of my self-sabotage patterns, but I was in information overload — another self-help book, another attachment theory, always a problem to be fixed. My mind was exploding, but my body could barely catch up.

There comes a point where self-awareness is actually self-judgment when there is no embodiment, and no integration period to process it all.

True healing isn't about fixing something broken; it's about remembering that you are whole and worthy exactly as you are.

The real problem isn't the guilt; the real problem is your mind is so full of information on how to fix it that you haven't taken a moment to process or integrate this emotion.

It's so much easier to distract suffering with intellect.

Our mind loves to understand and comprehend, but even if your brain makes sense of your distractions, you'll still pay the price until you go to the core — the body.

Count the hours you spent on courses, workshops, classes, and book after book for the last couple of years, and compare it to how much time you spent embodying, being, and processing what you learned in your body.

The only fixing that needs to happen is the speed at which you are consuming information.

Next time you want to Google why you're feeling down or tired, can you give your body five minutes to listen to what your inherent wisdom wants to tell you?

You have worked the mental part out in your mind, and the spiritual part out with your soul, but the home of your mind and soul is your body.

Embodiment is not healing; it's integrating what you already know.

Slowing down rather than fixing.

Being rather than planning.

Taking action with fear rather than journaling about it forever.

It's accessing empowerment from your own being rather than outsourcing it from outside of yourself from leaders, coaches, books, etc.

Embodiment isn't just another modality; it's all of them together.

Embodiment is the wake-up call to who the heck you are and came to this world for.

Embodiment gets you out of your mind and into the body, the present moment.

Remember, you already have everything you need within you. It's time to unleash it.

Courage

All the blood leaves my face. I feel my legs crumble underneath me.

I need to lie down.

I need the earth to swallow me up.

My life is over.

I am alone in a third-world country, and it's a ghost town in the streets.

I was lucky to find a doctor who would even see me. I had to travel an hour to get there by bus.

Lockdown had gotten so strict in the beach town in Panama I was in that there were only certain hours and days of the week you could leave your house.

This young doctor whispers in a low voice, "There are not many options, abortion is illegal in our country, you and I could go to jail."

I am so confused. I took Plan B as soon as I realized the condom broke. There must be an error on the pregnancy test. He looks at the blood test results and explains the growing ECG levels mean there is no mistake.

I walk alone back to the bus stop to the shared dorm, living out of a backpack.

I thought this was freedom.

Where did I mess up so bad?

I was continents away from my home and any family, and my bank account was too scary low to look at, in a situationship that I see absolutely no future with.

I decided to take a selfie to try to catch a glimpse of myself in my reflection.

I don't recognize the person on the screen.

"You are not alone," I said to myself, and this was the final step to gather the courage to call a mutual friend I knew was a life coach.

I put the voice that felt I could do it alone aside and asked her to guide me.

This call wasn't an ordinary call.

It was a call that killed parts of my ego clinging onto being able to do it all myself, smart to fix the problems I made for myself.

***

Three years later, I am a somatic empowerment coach with a thriving business, living on the island of my dreams, and I am calling the woman on the other side of that phone to invite her to my wedding.

There is so much unhealthy pride when it comes to growth and healing.

But true pride belongs to surrender.

It takes courage to let go of your thoughts until this point and to make room for something different, something outside of your own brain, beliefs, and patterns.

It takes courage to seek support, it takes courage to hire a mentor or healer, it takes courage to confront difficult emotions, it takes courage to have uncomfortable conversations with your loved ones.

There is someone today who is ready to take your call, ready to receive you, ready to listen, to hold space for you — but that step doesn't happen until you let go of the ego that wants to fix it all on its own.

Courage is illogical, so stop trying to think your way or convince your way into it and pick up the phone.

Self-Judgment

I crane my head to get a closer look at the sloth hanging upside down in the rainforest trees right above me.

It's a sunny humid day in the north of Costa Rica on a tour exploring the incredible wildlife.

I overheard a guide say something that completely blew my mind.

An American tourist was complaining there was something wrong with him because he couldn't see the sloth.

His tour guide responded, "Your eyes aren't bad. You're just not accustomed to seeing in this environment."

We're so quick to judge ourselves; if we can't see clearly, our eyes must be bad, if we can't hear then we have bad hearing, if we're not disciplined then we have bad habits, and if we struggle with emotions then we have bad mental health.

None of these are actually bad. You're just not accustomed to expressing it in this society.

We love to fix things when things aren't broken.

The guy on the tour was so fixated on seeing the sloth that when he didn't immediately see what he was looking for, it automatically meant something was wrong with him.

What if we spent less time trying to fix bad habits, bad emotions, and bad body sensations, and spent more time liberating this self-judgment so we actually had the capacity to see, feel, and act in a way that was present, not perfect?

There are no bad or good emotions, body sensations, or thoughts. These are all an experience of being human, of being alive.

It takes patience and commitment to accustom yourself to building the muscle of self-compassion so that you can fully feel.

Disbelief

I don't care how good your vision board is, you're still missing this one thing.

You can't receive the manifestations that your nervous system resists.

Before you do any manifestation or mindset work, train your body to actually be able to receive these incredible goals.

Your mind may want to make massive amounts of money, host sold-out retreats, and buy land to start your homestead...

But no amount of vision boarding will help, if on a deeper level your body doesn't believe it's possible.

Even a small sensation of disbelief or doubt is your nervous system protecting itself, and it will use all its energy to resist opportunities, courage, and commitment to make these goals possible.

To shift this on a body level, you transform the fear of doubt into the awe of amazement.

Disbelief and awe are two sides of the same coin; they are both simply unbelievable.

Invite the doubt in your body. Feel the contraction and tightness, and then move that same energy into amazement, astonishment, or awe.

Then choose one action to embody this shift.

Over time, when you devote yourself to channeling the energy of doubt into amazement, this will form your new belief.

Doubt

It's the same doubt in your body whether you're making $5,000 months or $50,000 months, so you might as well stretch your capacity for uncertainty.

When I was making $5,000 months, I was merging the world of embodiment and business, and I felt no one understood what somatics or nervous systems even were.

I had so much doubt if this was the direction I should pursue or if I should stick to what everyone understood — basic boring business.

What I did was welcome the doubt and fear of not being understood in my body and used it as fuel to build the muscle of trust. I didn't know if people would accept this concept of wealth and embodiment, so I CREATED the space for myself to belong, and from there was born an almost half-a-million-dollar global movement, Body Talk.

At the time of writing this book, I am making continuous $50,000 months. There is doubt that changemakers really understand how instrumental in-person somatic immersions really are to creating global impact.

So again, I welcome this doubt in my body and am creating a radical in-person event that feels so unknown, terrifying, and edgy. I have never seen it done before; I don't know if people will understand or get it, but I will only know if I create it.

The doubt doesn't go away; the muscle of taking action in the unknown simply continues to get stronger.

Doubt means you don't know, and therefore, you don't take that step.

Trust means you don't know, and because of that, you take the next step.

Basically, in order to trust yourself, you have to expand your capacity to experience doubt in your body.

That happens through action that feels terrifying, edgy, misunderstood, or different.

It's easy to trust when you are at a Cacao Ceremony with sound-healing bowls in the background.

It takes a lot of courage, strength, and devotion to trust to take action without knowing how it will be received, if people will join, and if it will be as successful as you hope.

Uncertainty is the pathway to certainty.

Misunderstood is the pathway to feeling understood.

Not being accepted is the pathway to acceptance.

The thing that you're running from feeling is the actual thing that brings your deepest desires.

To be able to trust yourself is to be able to hold yourself as you fall, not to never fall.

Pride

The hardest pill to swallow wasn't the valium I had to take for my anxiety for the first time in my life.

It was my pride.

I am a somatic coach. I am all natural and holistic, and I help my clients liberate heavy emotions.

I should have been able to just shake out my nerves before my wedding in an embodiment practice.

But with all the tools I had, I simply was not coping.

I was surrounded by all my friends and family, yet I could hardly breathe, eat, or sleep.

My body never experienced this amount of love and excitement and didn't know how to hold it all.

You can have all the tools, training, and certifications, but sometimes your body just hasn't caught up with your knowledge at this new level.

Often, we put ourselves on healing pedestals, that we shouldn't have this struggle if we have already overcome it before.

But life sometimes gives you situations where you are pushed to a new limit in order to prepare you for the deeper level of receiving and joy that you are about to step into.

In all the wedding planning that I did, there was all this information on how to budget, how to plan, and how to design and decorate, but no one talked about the mental and emotional wellbeing of the bride and groom.

It's just a given that on your big day, you will be the most nervous you have ever been and the happiest you have ever been, but most people's nervous systems do not know how to hold and carry these intense emotions at the same time.

On top of planning our entire destination wedding ourselves, we were also hosting family and friends who had never been to Mexico and didn't know the language.

Which meant organizing taxis, accommodation, SIM cards, lost suitcases, transportation, and housekeepers.

So by the time it was the morning of my wedding, I was running on three hours of sleep, and a tight chest full of intense emotions that I didn't know how to carry.

I messaged Hannah, the friend who is a powerful mystic and healer, and within thirty minutes, she was there doing the most intense and liberating release ceremony while I was getting my hair done.

I wish I had words to describe what happened, but in short, she saved my wedding.

I was able to be present, so happy, so energized, so me.

Everyone sees the dress, the hair and makeup, and the venue, but people never forget what they feel — the energy, the emotion, the love.

Polarity Practice

Take a picture on your phone, turn the brightness all the way up and you'll be blinded. Turn the shadows to the lowest extent, and you won't see anything either.

Positive thinking is great, but it can be blinding. Same as shadow work — too much darkness, and there is nothing the eye can pick up.

The light and dark in polarity practices do not mean good or bad, right or wrong.

They remove the moral compass and allow you to feel exactly what is present.

Through this, you are able to listen to the unique wisdom your body is sharing with you.

This is a language, your unique language, and in the beginning it may feel like learning the ABCs, but before you know it, it turns into words, then sentences, then a glorious expansive vocabulary that you feel so confident to express yourself in.

The capacity to learn a language begins with the choice of speaking the language every day.

Here is a *Body Talk* practice that will guide you to experience this chapter in your body.

Begin by becoming aware of any emotions, sensations, or feelings that are heavy, dark, or noisy for you.

Notice how it takes shape in your body: the posture, the breath, the shape, the movements, the way it wants to move, take up space. The speed, the texture, whether it's high up or low down, facial expressions, sounds.

The capacity to fully feel it will allow you to deeply hear what your body is saying.

We will call this Character A.

Is it slouched down or sharp and straight?

Is it super small or tall and massive?

Is the breath feeling tight or fast?

What type of posture does it have? Which way is the spine curving, inwards or straight?

Try exaggerating that shape.

Imagine you are in theater practice, and you're given the handout of a character. This isn't you, this is a character you are taking on.

How do they dress, walk, talk, and take up space in the room?

What are their facial expressions? Are they annoyed or tired?

What does Character A wish to say, if it could say anything? What's the first thing that comes out of its mouth? It doesn't need to make sense. What is it asking for, perhaps even begging for?

Take a couple of moments to speak, move, and express the full expression of this Character A that has become present in this practice.

Amazing.

Take a breath, a little shake, and thank Character A for allowing us to explore them.

Now, we are going to invite a second character to play.

This is Character B. This is the other end of the spectrum, the light of the shadow, the desire of the fear.

Invite Character B into your body now.

In relation to this practice, this emotion, this block, what is the desire, the light, the possibility?

Again, we begin with breath.

How does Character B want to breathe? Is it light, is an exhale, is it gentle?

What's happening to their facial expressions? Is there a softness, a smile?

Do the eyes want to be open or closed?

Let's look at the heart space. Does it feel open? Expanded?

How about the shoulders? Do they feel strong or restful?

Invite a hum, a sound, or vibration from the throat.

What sound does Character B make? High-pitched, playful, majestic?

When Character B feels ready, we are going to invite it to stand up and take up space in the room. What type of steps live here: gentle, powerful, jumping, dancing?

How does Character B feel in this state? Alive, energized, excited?

What do they want to say? The first thing is exactly it; there's no way to get this wrong.

Beautiful.

Take a breath and now invite back in Character A, and this time you get to play both characters.

Give each a space in the room, and let them face one another.

Embody Character A looking up or towards Character B. If it could say what it really wanted to say, what would that be? This character can be angry, resentful, sad, or begging. Let it express what a character (not your mind) would want to say.

Move now to Character B, their posture, facial expression, and sensations. Without any fixing or changing the other character, what does it wish to respond to Character A?

We are going to repeat this, going back and forth at least three times to open up a dialogue between these two parts that live within your body.

What does one want from the other? How do they wish to co-create or work together?

You can choose now to freeform write any messages that came through, any ahas, any ways you can have deeper compassion or use the fear as fuel today.

This gets to be your devotion of the day.

Sometimes, it can feel very clear, other times super vague.

The power lives in the action you choose to take from the practice and make that your devotion for the day.

Here is an example of what this practice can look like:

Character A is rejection, and Character B is deep self-trust.

In the dialogue, rejection asked for reassurance.

The action could be reassuring yourself through celebrating how far you have come and sharing in your stories a picture of you a year ago and all the courage and steps you took to get to where you are today.

The rejection has turned into fuel, creating a snowball effect of creative energy and being in the state of receiving.

	Character A	Character B
Body		
Key Phrase		
What does it really want?		
Liberated Message/request of the body		

Part II: Self-Expression

Give this language a voice

What is self – expression?

I'm about to board a one-way ticket to Africa.

I kiss my mother on the cheek.

My heart aches a little. I want to stay warm and cozy in her embrace forever and never leave her side.

I'm 21, a young, ultra-orthodox Jewish girl, and there were a lot of people in the community with opinions about this crazy trip I was about to embark on.

It's not that I don't care about what people think.

It's just that I care more about the life I want to live than whatever people are saying about me.

So, I took all this judgment and gossip and decided to create my own story instead of others creating it for me.

I started to share my travels through blog posts and on my social media, and slowly grew my account with many Jewish girls just like me who also loved traveling, and through watching my content, they built the courage to go on trips and adventures themselves even when it wasn't common.

Fear of judgment means you care what people think about you.

The whole reason you do this is because you deeply care.

It doesn't help anyone to stop caring. Rather, choose to care MORE about the impact you are making.

If you numb yourself to caring what people think, you are also numbing yourself to caring deeply about the people whose lives are changing through your message.

You get to channel your empathy into caring more about the impact you are creating than the judgements people will have about you.

The way you do this is by feeling and experiencing the fear, the frustration, and the doubt in your throat.

Either you care what people think, letting their expectations run your life, OR you care more about the impact you are creating and share your message.

This chapter explores all the fears that come up when you create, express, and share your story, and how it's an opportunity to give your body the microphone.

Creating content gives your fear a voice, an opportunity to be seen and heard.

Content gives your soul a voice so it can speak in this 3D physical world we live in.

Art is your soul communicating through you.

When you post your art,

share your videos,

release a podcast episode,

talk on your Instagram stories,

publish your poems,

you are allowing the divine to express itself through you.

I studied all the best marketing strategies. I bought better camera equipment. I spent hours editing my photos and videos.

It took me seven years of consistent content creation to figure out that there was no secret strategy.

The best marketing strategy is to listen and express what your body is saying.

If you want your content to make an impact and to convince people all across the world to invest in your products and services, you need your content to make them FEEL something.

When you describe something as "touching" or "moving," it's quite literally the sensation of touch or being moved in your body.

On social platforms, we like, share, comment, engage, and ultimately buy when we feel something.

We continue scrolling when we feel nothing, when we feel numb.

In a noisy digital world, it's more important than ever to learn how to tell your story better, to connect with your body and your emotions, and to create in a way that connects deeply to the person on the other side of the screen.

Creativity is spirituality, and this magical energy does not live in the 5D, it lives in the "post" button, the "publish" button, the "upload" button.

This chapter will guide you in liberating your unique voice and the language of your body so that you can effectively share your message with the world.

When you create body-based content, you give your fear a voice and an opportunity to be heard. In order for your audience to feel something from your content, you need the capacity to feel that thing first in your own body, and then express it from that state of activation.

Attention

It's pouring rain, and the path ahead makes a sharp turn. I press the brakes so hard and fast on the bike I'm riding that I fly a whole 360 degrees and land flat on my face.

I'm 13, and it was my first time at school camp.

School was a really lonely place for me. I had no friends. I cried for months. Eventually, I shut off all my emotions and became completely numb.

Up until this day, I was invisible.

Now everywhere I went, people stared.

My lip was busted, there were gashes across my forehead, and I was covered in bruises.

I had two choices: to hide even deeper in my pain, or to take the attention and turn it into my superpower.

I chose to take the attention, no matter how uncomfortable it was.

I told my story. I broke out of my shell. I showed my personality. No one had known I was funny, that I could be the life of the party when I chose to.

That decision changed my life.

In high school, being amazing at receiving attention earned me courage, a social circle, and the best memories.

In business, being amazing at receiving attention earned my methodology to become renowned and allowed me to build a movement that impacts thousands.

Attention is the number one currency.

Instagram is free, but it makes billions of dollars because it sells attention.

Ads bring in millions by catching your attention.

You can be the most incredible coach, but until you master the art of attention, people with half the skill will gain all the clients and therefore, the impact.

Traditional marketing teaches you how to speak to your audience's mind.

But to be known, to be memorable, to be chosen out of thousands of others in the industry happens when you tap into the core primal sensation of attention.

Real attention speaks to your audience's body, to their feelings, sensations, and emotions.

There's nothing wrong with desiring popularity, with desiring attention, with wanting all eyes on you.

Being seen is a primal desire.

It becomes messy when we attach meaning to it.

It becomes confusing when we make metrics personal.

It becomes needy when we rely on views for dopamine.

If we were honest with ourselves and claimed our brilliance, we would flirt with social media instead of fighting for our place in this noisy digital world.

Your content is your opportunity to be a flirt, to lick your lips, and invite your audience into your delicious world.

Some teasing in your offers, eye contact in your Instagram lives, confidence seeping out of your voice.

You don't need many words to flirt. Your body does most of the talking.

You don't need a lesson in content.

You need a reminder from your teenage self on how to flirt with your desires.

It's time to embody the version of you that is so seductive that your audience is sitting on the edge of their seats, drooling at the opportunity to work with you.

Your audience doesn't need your fake humility keeping you polite, quiet, and cozy in the corner.

If you really want to make a massive impact and be widely known for your voice, it's time to:

Claim your boldness.

Claim your unique gifts.

Claim your epic story.

Claim your powerful offers.

Feminine

Embodied women are the best at creating wealth because money is feminine.

Growing up in a Jewish household, my dad being a Rabbi for our community, I was very connected to God and spirituality. I especially felt connected to Chassidut, the teaching of Kabbalah, experiencing the divine in our physical world.

In Kabbalah, the feminine part of the soul represents receiving the channels of the divine flow in the physical world.

When I was younger, the role of the woman would bother me. To me, the woman felt less important because she was the receiver, and at the time, receiving felt like pity or passiveness.

As I began to dive deeper into these teachings and build a global movement that impacts thousands, I realized that I had the feminine all confused.

The feminine is not passive; she is the creator!

While the feminine naturally is receiving, I realized this doesn't make her less than; rather, it empowers her as a creator of channels through which abundance flows.

The feminine is the creator. She creates these channels through art, voice, expression, beauty, and desire.

This is why embodied women are the best at creating wealth, because they create the container to receive abundance through CREATION.

Sharing your voice, and expressing who you really are attracts dream clients and opportunities to you. This doesn't mean dancing around in a flowy dress barefoot and you will make millions. It means creating the channels by bringing beauty and art into the world, and you will magnetize the wealth to you.

The feminine is the receiving energy, the attraction energy, the excited, flirty, desire-based energy in your body.

But the biggest mistake lies in passive receiving.

"I'm beautiful, so someone will ask me out," — without ever going out on a date.

"I have an amazing offer, so my clients will find me," — without creating an experience that gives your audience a taste of working with you.

Feminine energy is not passive.

She doesn't just lie there wishing and waiting.

The feminine is the CREATOR. She creates through art, beauty, desire, words, expression, and attraction.

Match your desires with your creations.

You want selling to feel playful?

CREATE games and fun experiences that your community can interact with.

You want to make more money that feels meaningful?

CREATE meaning by sharing your story and going deeper with your community.

Chaos

I woke up the day after turning 30 feeling all over the place. I was up for hours because of jetlag and recovering from feeling nauseous and disappointed because the world-famous Na Pali Coast Boat Tour was canceled because of strong winds.

My body was churning, my mind felt dizzy, and in the middle of all the chaos, I received a message from a client on the other side of the world that my unique method was changing the game for so many of her clients!

That's when it clicked.

I was traveling to experience the most incredible views in Kauai while clients all over the globe were getting incredible transformations from my Body Talk method.

"All over the place" was my body, preparing me for being world renowned, known across the globe for my unique method.

My day could have just been sleepy, nauseous, and feeling sorry for myself that I was 30 and didn't have it all together.

But instead, I took that chaotic, unsteady energy and decided, "I AM ALL OVER THE PLACE!"

I am literally in Hawaii, and my clients all across the world are using my unique method to change people's lives.

I am all over the internet with my content, and thousands of women across the globe are gaining so much value from my workshops.

At every moment, you have a choice. Your body is communicating with you your biggest wisdom.

You get to choose to allow it to hold you back or to turn it into the thing that changes the world.

All over the place is a superpower if you allow it to be.

I see so many coaches and mentors spending hours trying to think their way into clarity, but the truth is, before your wisdom finds its way into words, it lives as a message in your body.

If you know your work is powerful and you want to translate the magic of your sessions into content that actually makes someone feel, try this out:

> *Before trying to write up that fiery caption, find the feeling this message has in your body.*
>
> *Even if you have all the self-development and meditation tools, without movement, without embodiment, all that wisdom stays hidden and blocked in the body.*
>
> *If you want to move someone on the other side of the screen to tears, to action, to invest with you, it starts with actually moving your own body.*
>
> *To liberate your voice is to learn the language of your body and then express it from that space.*

Hypocrisy

I am in an expensive lobby in Zambia. I walk past a spread of delicacies at a high tea, through the foyer, and past incredible manicured gardens. I lead my friend with calm and assured eyes, nodding to her, "Follow my lead," as we reach a beautiful pool overlooking the nature reserves.

Her eyes widen as we watch the monkeys and elephants in the distance. I could sense her getting fidgety, and her body stiffen as staff would walk by. I gave her the eye, reminding her of my instructions as we left our pitched pink tent at the hostel in town that we paid under $5 for.

In my 20s, my favorite magic trick as a budget backpacker was to walk with my head up so confidently into the most luxurious resorts around the world as if I were a paying guest.

It worked every time; I had it down to a science.

"If you believe you belong, everyone will believe it as well."

When I first started coaching, I was not good at getting clients interested in working with me.

I was a marketing coach and knew I was amazing at my job. I had been a digital nomad for six years and worked in creating content and social media management for other businesses.

But when it came to promoting my own work, there was this itchiness in my skin, a stiffening in my body, my eyes widening with doubt.

It felt like I had to force or convince people into wanting to work with me.

It felt so hypocritical. How could I coach people on something that I was struggling with myself?

I had the skills. I was freaking talented and knowledgeable.

But the gap wasn't my skills; it was my capacity to believe how powerful my offers were and experience full-body conviction that I was the one for them.

Having the best skills, wisdom, and certifications isn't enough.

You have to have the audacity to truly believe that what you have to share is powerful enough to promote and share with the world.

You have to believe in yourself so much to hurt your ego's pride and connect to a deeper sense of pride from within.

***

I am standing barefoot, leaving a sandy trail at an important-looking office overlooking the most insane view of the Dominican Republic's blue ocean and five-star boutique hotel.

I am holding my trusty tripod and my backpack with my drone and camera. I gently knock, and a voice says, "Come in."

A man and woman are sitting at the desk. They thank me and hand me $500 cash.

On the outside, they are paying for a video I filmed for their website, but what is actually happening is they are paying me for simply believing that I belonged there.

I am 23, and I walk down the road to my shared dorm room where I am an animation dancer at the resort next door. I laugh to myself because I just made my monthly paycheck on my off day swimming in the most beautiful infinity pools.

I became so good at believing I belonged at the most beautiful resorts that I actually had the audacity to whip out my trusty camera, take some incredible content, and walk up to find a manager and get paid for believing I belonged there.

> *Belief is a choice.*

> *Belief is a daily practice.*

> *What would you say today if you truly believed that your message would impact someone's life?*

> *How would you express yourself if you believed you didn't believe you were the one?*

> *How would you take up space?*

> *Provide value versus tip-toeing around your desires.*

Depression

I am 10 years old, and the birds are singing outside. It's barely 6am, and I wake up in a panic.

I hear noises downstairs. My father is leaving to go to Synagogue. I wait until I hear his car leave. I creep downstairs, and I hide in my father's bed. An hour rolls by, and the house begins to wake up. I can hear my sisters having breakfast. I sink deeper into the mattress. I am invisible. If I hold my breath, no one will find me.

The van starts piling up with kids.

"Sheinaaaaa."

I hear my name being called. They are already running late.

"Not again, Sheina, let's gooo."

I hear some scurried sounds as my older sister searches for me. I have different hiding spots every day. The pain in my chest feels like I am going to pass out.

"We're leaving Sheina," I hear.

Tiny exhale.

I hear the van leave the driveway; a little more air escapes my lungs.

I try going back to sleep to take away the pain in my heart.

My mom doesn't try to convince me to go to the new school. I had just abruptly been moved from a small Jewish day school that my father ran, to a massive school with hundreds of girls, which made my tummy feel like it was being attacked in every direction.

I was so confused by this sudden change. I felt like I was snatched out of my life.

I've got a feeling that my mother is the only one in the world who can understand my aching heart because I see the way she hides from the pain, too.

***

I'm 30 years old, and my body feels ice cold. I'm digging deeper and deeper into my covers, hoping to disappear. It feels like the world has stopped.

Our beautiful puppy had just run away. We were on our Shabbat walk to Synagogue, a little too confident that Callie, our wedding present from a friend a couple of months earlier, was ready to walk without her leash like she had done so well the previous night and many times before.

The ache was burning in my chest. I couldn't breathe. I couldn't see anyone. I locked myself in my room while Kfir, my new husband, spent days in the jungle searching for Callie.

I am sitting on my couch like a piece of stone in a dark house; I didn't even realize it had become night time.

I see a shooting star from where I'm sitting.

Time stops. The falling feels like an eternity.

I hear a wail.

That sound came out of me.

My body realizes that Callie is not in our world anymore. My stone heart feels like it is shattering into a million pieces.

I cry for the dog I allowed my heart to fall in love with.

I cry for the 10-year-old who got so good at hiding from her pain.

I cry for my mother, who carries all of our pain.

I cry for my grandmothers who had no other options but to push the pain deep down and continue on with their brave faces and carry the weight of the ones they loved.

For the first time in my life, I actually invited the sensation of deep grief to penetrate my body without hiding.

For the first time, I understand you are supposed to feel depressed.

***

I used to be terrified of depression. It stole so much of my childhood.

Depression was a constant guest in my childhood home.

It kept the person I loved most physically close but mentally so, so distant. So naturally, depression became the enemy.

Whenever the feeling arrived, I avoided feeling it at all costs. I preferred to feel nothing than to feel the heaviness in my chest.

For years, I even avoided saying the word because it was too extreme, too dark, too heavy, too painful.

The thing is, depression isn't the problem. It's our fear that we'll get stuck there that is actually what keeps us stuck.

I allowed myself to continue feeling the somatic sensation of depression over the next few weeks as the pain moved through my body.

The sound of the wail turned into powerful poems, gentle somatic practices for my clients, heart-to-heart podcast episodes, and cathartic in-person somatic immersions.

A raw deep level of empathy and capacity to deeply feel my clients while powerful facilitating emerged.

Your voice is the medicine for your pain.

When you share your voice, you allow this pain to move through your body and transform into your legacy.

Intuition

It kind of pisses me off when coaches confuse intuition with doing what feels good.

What feels good in the body isn't actually what is good for you.

It feels good to eat a box of candy at the moment, but that feeling doesn't last long.

If intuition were always a good feeling in the body, then all the changemakers would just be watching, wishing, and waiting.

It feels good, cozy, and comfortable to play small.

It feels nourishing to be needy, dependent, and not take responsibility.

Trusting your intuition when building a business that changes the world actually doesn't feel great a lot of the time.

It can feel terrifying, it can feel nauseating, it can feel painful.

Trust happens when you take action with that discomfort in the body rather than fix it.

The difference between fear and intuition in your body is more than a somatic shake or breathwork practice.

It's the capacity to deeply learn the language of what your body is saying — letting your body talk and express yourself rather than trying to calm down and regulate your nervous system.

Giving your fear a voice through sharing your message online IS how you can actually tell the difference between fear and intuition.

This took me years to figure out, but your life doesn't have to be glamorous or entertaining to tell YOUR story. People want to see the real, raw you. Your life is more interesting when you stop comparing it to someone else's and start comparing your today to your last year.

This is what makes storytelling different from any other art form.

Everyone has a story, and you don't have to be talented in order to share it.

Storytelling is the most accessible form of art.

It's not a strategy, not a trending audio, not a specific tripod brand.

The only thing getting in the way of you telling your story is how worthy you feel around sharing your voice.

People don't want to be helped; they want to be activated. If your content doesn't give your audience chills or some emotional or bodily reaction, how do you expect them to be excited to work with you?

I have nothing against journaling, but if you really want to articulate your wisdom and find the right words to express your powerful message, you've got to move your body.

Don't create content to get more followers.

Create content for leaders.

Your audience is the empowered creators of their reality, not sheep that follow the herd.

Your followers aren't stupid.

They don't fit into a box of hooks and catchy trends.

They're unique thinkers who don't spend their time on social media as bait, waiting to be saved by some guru who will change their lives.

Your content should speak to leaders, to powerful people who desire to grow, not to people waiting to be saved. Your audience is ready to take massive action and invest with you, so treat them as massive action-takers with the content that you create for them!

Don't let finding your voice be an excuse to get even more lost in your mind.

Consistency

You don't have a consistency problem. You are just motivated by fear instead of desire.

The self-growth experts will convince you the key to success is consistency, but as someone who has been creating and posting consistently for years, I can tell you that's not the complete truth.

When you create because you fear failure, fear rejection, fear disappointing yourself, it's like trying to row in the opposite direction of the river.

You will get tired very quickly and annoyed as you watch all the other boats floating with such ease.

The whole internet is full of 'consistency is key,' but if your body hasn't caught up to where your mind is, you'll just consistently be doing the things that don't actually get you where you want to go.

When your content is fueled by your deep desire to create, to express, to share, to teach, to make a difference, suddenly, you're in a flow state.

There is poetry pouring out of your mouth, there are DMs filled with lives who have been impacted by your posts, there are the dreamiest clients that are excited to work with you, there are opportunities landing everywhere.

When you BECOME the version of yourself that creates because of a pure desire to share and express, showing up on social media is like creating art because you're no longer trying to be someone you're not.

Lack of consistency isn't what is going to hurt you. Being driven by fear will.

Confusion

The idea of impacting thousands of people is incredible, but how many of you will go through what it takes to press record thousands of times?

How many reps are you willing to put in to train your nervous system for the day you will sell out festivals, retreats, conferences, events, and life-changing programs?

How many times will you pour your heart and soul on live whether or not anyone is not responding?

What's your capacity to continue overflowing value into your community as if there were 100 people there even when there are 10?

What's your capacity to host workshop after workshop, to continually be excited about what you have to share, to continually promote and invite when it feels like too much.

What's your capacity for people to have different views than you, to disagree with what you have to say, to be disappointed in what they paid for, to try to challenge you? Having hundreds in your groups does not take more strategy; it takes more emotional mastery to be with more fear as your groups grow.

You don't need to wait to be confident to serve hundreds of people in your containers.

You BECOME confident as you embrace confusion and have a play-date with chaos.

Allowing yourself to experiment, to try again, to experience the embarrassment of not getting it 100% on the first try is the pathway.

Your nervous system won't love it, it prefers to take it easy and stay in the safety net of being distracted.

If you want to use your voice and become widely known for your story and wisdom, you have to let go of your grip of needing to fit your whole identity neatly and clearly in the grid of social media.

Feeling confused about your message is your body asking you to accept your multi-passionate self.

It's asking you to celebrate the real, the raw, the messy, the in-between, and, dare I say, imperfect.

You can be into fashion AND wellness. You can be into health AND intuition — the only thing stopping your authenticity is your firm grip on fitting into the box of fully ready, fully clear, fully embodied, fully expert, and fully confident.

Instead of waiting to share when you feel clear and confident in your purpose on social media, share today what's alive for you at this moment.

Be a voice in this noisy world by being courageous enough to put in the reps of confusion.

Potential

I'm just going to say it: You keep hiding behind your screen, splashing the words *embodiment and empowerment* in your content, but behind the scenes, you are feeling embarrassed and behind.

Your mind may have done all the inner work, but your body is holding onto the shame of not living your full potential or not being at the level you should be.

Embodiment does not mean you are living your fullest, most expanded, conscious, abundant, regulated nervous system life.

Embodiment is your capacity to process shame blocked in your body and transform it into your superpower.

When your shame is suppressed in the body, it turns into bad habits, doom scrolling, not keeping your promises to yourself.

When shame is liberated, it turns into powerful storytelling and impactful offers, building a movement where people feel seen and a sense of belonging.

Your story holds the key to massive success, and while you sit here complaining of how slow your growth is, there is a past version of you wishing they had even a few minutes with you for guidance and clarity.

That's the purpose of your shame — to be the glimmer, the permission slip, the reminder for others who are really just a mirror of who you used to be.

So, instead of sharing some wordy post about living your dream life, go on live today and share real words about living your real life today!

Because for many, that is the dream life they are working towards.

Niche

Stop trying to fit into a niche when you are the whole goddamn GENRE!

If you feel confused about how to introduce yourself, how to find the words to explain what you do, and how to express your message online coherently, this is a sign that you're a pioneer.

Confusion is the way your body tells you to stop putting yourself into boxes or titles.

You are unique; you are different.

You don't fit into a neat category, a title, or a niche because you are the whole goddamn genre!

You spend hours thinking, *Am I a marketing coach, or am I a healing coach? Am I an interior designer, or am I a social media manager?*

Girl, you are not a title, and you will never fit into one!

To be the genre is to create a new pathway.

This requires you to do things that have never been done before.

THIS WILL FEEL CONFUSING IN YOUR NERVOUS SYSTEM!

You write and rewrite your posts so many times, you overthink and overanalyze your words, and even then, it hardly does justice to the powerful work that you do...

This is a sign your mind is trying to control, which makes you feel frustrated with yourself.

This is why it's so important to create embodied content, to listen to your emotions as guides so that you can express and articulate in a way that activates your audience!

We tend to chase clarity as salvation.

In reality, when you expand your capacity to experience confusion in your body, you can expand your capacity to experience clarity!

You don't have a niche problem; you have a nice problem.

You're terrified of being disliked, and you are people-pleasing all over your audience.

You can help this person, and you can also help them, and you wouldn't dare exclude that person — that wouldn't be nice.

The reason why your content isn't reaching your dream clients, the reason why your income isn't feeling consistent, is because you're being too nice.

Your content is vague and broad because you're hiding behind the fear of being disliked.

Look at your favorite clients. What do they have in common?

What lights your soul on fire the most when you teach?

Share that thing with all your heart.

This isn't a life sentence; this is the present moment.

It's not going to fit in a box; you're not going to get it 'perfect' or right, but it's going to talk directly to the 'right' person.

When you start sharing in this way, you are going to deter some people, perhaps even some clients, but to be magnetic is to be both a force of attraction and repulsion.

It's easy to say you can handle being disliked, but can your nervous system actually handle it?

Fear

Summer in New York has a distinct smell. We just landed. I am sweaty and sleepy and I can't wait to have a relaxing evening with friends by the pool.

Kfir has other plans and gives me an excited look, "We're going dirt bike riding," he says.

There is no way he is convincing me to get on a bike, I assure myself.

***

I am standing in line to go ATV riding at summer camp. I am 8 years old.

All the kids are confidently putting on their helmets and going around this simple path around the size of the oval we run around on sports day.

I squint my eyes, tracking my friend who just went before me.

My turn arrives. I am given a helmet. I hear some instructions. Start, stop, speed on the turns. I can feel my heart start to quicken. Wait. Slow down. Say that again. This is confusing. I must have said that to myself because the instructor thinks I'm ready to go.

I gulp.

It's really hot under this helmet, and it feels like a brick is sitting on my head. There's a line of kids waiting their turn.

I take a breath and turn the throttle.

I am so busy looking at my hands and figuring out what to press that I don't see the gate getting closer and closer to me.

I hear someone screaming. I lift my head. I see a gate. I feel a crash. I am on the ground with a heavy machine on me. My legs feel shaky. I feel so embarrassed everyone watched me drive straight into a wall.

***

I blink. I'm not 8 anymore, but my legs feel weak watching Kfir and his friend have the time of their lives riding dirt bikes around in the woods.

I know this is the perfect opportunity to expand my capacity to hold fear in my body, which is exactly how I guide my clients to embody courage.

To Kfir's joy, I told him I would give it a try.

Within ten minutes of guidance, my body became so in tune and focused on the new skill, and my brain became a powerful partner.

Instead of screaming DANGER, the fear was liberated into courage and pride.

Embodiment isn't about facing your fear — you can face your fears daily and be overwhelmed with anxious thoughts and a body stuck in freeze mode.

Instead, you want to expand your body's capacity to hold that fear, to process it, to embody it and only then that fear gets to be liberated.

You can't think, meditate, journal, or force your way through fears; you have to train the muscles in your body to hold and process that fear.

It is not about jumping in the deep end and just doing what scares you, it's about training your body to feel this fear to liberate it into courage.

Activation

Your body gives you an unfair advantage when growing your social media.

Content is an emotional exchange, and the home of your emotions is your body.

The more in tune and connected you are to your body, the deeper you can connect and relate with your audience.

Have you ever been scrolling and you get that sensation, a shiver up your spine, a quickening of your heartbeat? That's activation.

When you create from your mind, for example, 'what you think you should be posting,' you connect to the minds of your audience.

The mind questions, it rationalizes, it consumes information, and adds it to the already overflowing stash of noise in the brain.

When you create from your body 'what feels alive in your system right now' and listen to the messages your emotions are communicating to you, your content makes your audience feel something.

They feel activated, they feel belonging, they feel a sense of hopefulness and possibility for themselves, and sometimes they feel triggered, annoyed, confused, snapping them out of their patterns.

When your audience feels activated, they take action. Stop letting your mind rule the show and give a moment for your body, emotions, and inner wisdom to take the driver's seat.

Nauseous

I feel some throw-up sitting on the edge of my throat, ready to come out.

I feel so disgusted

I'm surrounded by a group of guys at a hostel.

"Dance for me," one of them says as the rest egg him on.

This cute guy I was talking to started following me on Instagram and saw that I traveled and danced around the world and wanted to see it in action.

A part of me had a crush on the guy and wanted to impress him. But my body was feeling extremely uncomfortable and humiliated.

I felt like a monkey in a cage just being used for entertainment.

It only comes out authentically when it comes from you, not as a need to please or perform or, even worse, pay the bills.

Your creativity goddess hides when there is an expectation tied to her.

Your creativity goddess gets nauseous when numbers and metrics are tied to her.

What if you created to create, to liberate your throat chakra, and as a by-product, the numbers followed suit?

Embody the transformation you are selling in front and behind the camera. Are you actually being the living message that you are sharing? Show that to your audience and to yourself when no one is watching.

Actually be the healthy diet, or the positive mindset, or the powerful leader of your own life.

People don't care about another inspirational quote or another thing they can learn about a subject. They care about the person living that quote, the person living the lesson they are teaching.

Tell your story, what you achieved, what you overcame, how you did it, and what steps took you there.

Storytelling is the most ancient form of connection, and in a world where people get so lost in screen time and comparison, they crave a sense of being related to, a sense of resonating with an emotion or feeling.

As Elizabeth Gilbert says in her book, *Big Magic,* "What do you love doing so much that the words *failure* and *success essentially* become irrelevant?" That is the actual secret to being seen.

Create as an art, an expression — not for a result.

Worthy

I don't want to be rich to live in a mansion and buy designer bags. I want to be rich so that I can wake up in a tent on an island, impacting thousands through my business while having the time of my life with my family present in nature.

Which is exactly why I find myself waking up in a tent overlooking the Pacific Ocean while making more money than my mind can even fathom.

I reflect on the time I took my business so seriously.

My worth was attached to my productivity and my clients' results. My body was carrying the weight of the world and all the responsibilities that come with it.

But after deep somatic work and addressing these beliefs at their core, I realized something profound:

Changing the world isn't that serious.

Making money isn't that serious.

When I started treating my business as a game where I was the winner in every scenario, everything transformed.

A launch not going to plan? Ten points for an opportunity to discover my next success code.

Someone disagreeing with my views on social media? Three points for standing firm in my beliefs.

A DM not responding? Five points for creating content that truly resonates.

Getting kicked out of my own workshop with 70 women on Zoom due to internet issues? Thirteen points for embodying resilience and managing overwhelm.

Business being fun isn't just a mindset shift; it's an active choice that transforms your belief system.

Your worth is inherent, but your worthiness of receiving a lot of money is something learned on a body level.

The most enjoyable way to teach your nervous system this is to treat it like a game and have fun playing.

You don't deserve to travel and enjoy your life because you worked hard for it; you inherently deserve it, period.

Society teaches us to work 50 weeks a year to earn a 2-week vacation, leading to burnout as we attach our worth to external achievements. We've been conditioned to believe we must earn our worth.

How many times have you said, "I can spoil myself because I worked hard; I deserve it."

To truly feel worthy of traveling whenever you desire and having a fulfilling business, you must reprogram your mind and body to recognize your inherent worth, unattached to results or rewards.

What if you created this inner worth, where the act of expression itself was enough, not measured by likes or views? What if you launched offers simply because they ignite your passion, not to hit a money goal but because sharing them lit your heart on fire?

Selling with joy and play, even if no one joined, where the act of promoting something you're passionate about was enough. These micro-moments of letting the act of expressing and sharing what you love be enough are the pathway to your body feeling deserving of your deepest desires.

If you want financial abundance like the abundance found in nature:

SERVE IN ABUNDANCE, CARE IN ABUNDANCE, GIVE IN ABUNDANCE, CREATE IN ABUNDANCE.

You don't deserve to change thousands of lives just because you are an amazing coach. You earn global impact by helping more people. You have as many followers as people you are activating. You have as much income as the lives you are changing.

This isn't about quality vs. quantity; it's about serving or not serving.

An impactful coach helps more people.

Motivation doesn't change lives; serving does.

Go on Instagram Live to guide your audience through a journey, even if you fear you might annoy them because you care more about the lives your gifts will help than the discomfort of being too much.

Commit to selling every day, even when you don't need the money because you care more about the ripple effect of your offers than the resistance of appearing needy.

Your nervous system's capacity to deeply help more people comes from caring MORE about the possibility of impact than the discomfort of fear or resistance.

Embarrassed

I feel my cheeks going bright red and my heart rate quickening.

I am sitting at a Friday night dinner with my best friends in Hawaii. This lovely woman approached our table and said, "Hey I follow you on Instagram," and proceeded to tell me about a certain post that had impacted her.

It felt so exhilarating, and I felt so seen.

I realized that this feeling in my body was similar to the moment a couple of years earlier...

***

It's November 2020, and almost all states are still in lockdown or social distancing, but it was my best friend's bachelorette, and there was no way she was having a boring party.

So, five of us got on a plane from the cold East Coast to sunny Florida, where we could dance the night away without getting dirty looks.

For some reason, we decided after our big night in town, we would wake up early and go to a private pole dance class, because why not?

We were sitting in an Uber, all bruised and out of breath from the class, and I told my friends I spent $3,000 on a course and I was going to become a coach.

Radio silence.

I think even the Uber driver was holding his breath.

Then came the million questions.

> *Who, you? A coach. We love you but you have hardly kept a job in the past five years.*
>
> *How are you going to teach other people how to live their dream lives and make money on the internet? You work in a mall selling skincare?*

Straight away, the blood came up to my cheeks. I could feel myself getting hot and stumbling on my words. I didn't have answers. There was no logic. This was a dream.

Heck, I could hardly understand why I wanted this so badly, but I knew with complete certainty that I was going to create a life for myself that I was obsessed with. I knew I would dance every day and travel the world. The pathway was not clear at all, though.

I took that shame and responded, "Watch me. I'm ready to try, I'm ready to experiment, I'm ready to learn and continue growing, and that will never end."

This hot sensation in my cheeks was the same when I was recognized or questioned. My nervous system didn't know the difference between the flush of attention and the flush of not being understood.

If I tried pushing down the sensation and hiding when I felt embarrassed, I wouldn't be recognized and thanked thousands of miles away from where I live.

Shame is a powerful emotion that keeps many of us small and scared but in reality, shame is your superpower when liberated and given a voice.

Shame doesn't only want to be heard when it is pretty and powerful, it wants to be seen in the ugly, it wants unconditional acceptance for the sticky in-between times.

I was embarrassed when I started my business. I had many streaks of 'failed' business attempts before. I was worried about taking up space because it's easier to fail silently with no one knowing, than failing while people watch.

But instead, I listened to the shame. It was asking permission to fail, it was asking permission to experience trial and error, it was asking me if I would have my own back no matter the result.

It's not enough to just journal about your experiences.

Your shame wants to be <u>seen and heard. It wants to be witnessed and accepted by you fully.</u>

I became recognized on the internet and in real life, personalities with millions of followers reposting my content not because it was perfect and professional, but because it was real and made my audience feel something.

Your capacity to be laughed at, ignored, misunderstood, and invisible is your capacity to be known, to be recognized, to be respected.

You can train your nervous system to transform the pain of being different into the fuel of pioneering the way to be known for something unique.

You don't have to hide the fact that you want to be recognized in public!

But you do have to come to terms with being recognized, which means you are different. You need to expand your capacity for the pain of standing out.

Don't apologize for being different. Make it what you become known for.

Being invisible is hard. Being unapologetically expressed is hard. Choose your hard.

I was laughed at until I was respected.

I was ignored until I was remembered.

I was ghosted until I was sought after.

I was invisible until I was recognized.

Confidence

" I'm going to look so different from everyone in the room..."

I stand nervously in front of the mirror. In an hour, I am speaking at a conference in front of 200 women, and my entire system is terrified.

I caught a good look at my posture, my body language, and my sunken shoulders.

I caught the pattern living in my body: *Stay quiet, don't make a scene, don't ask for trouble.*

The moment I stood crouching in the mirror I caught years worth of conditioning living in my body to try to fit into the crowd.

In school, people would call me an attention seeker and teachers always make sure my voice would be contained.

The thing about claiming the stage, is you have to transform the conditioning that gets stored in the body, that experiences receiving a lot of attention as arrogant, annoying, or even something you'll get punished for.

I had a choice in the morning between two dresses. One would fit in, be more casual, and not cause stares or too much attention.

The other was a silk, white, open-back dress that looked like it belonged on a runway.

I made a choice in that moment to be proud of getting attention for being different.

I chose to claim the stage even if I was the smallest fish in the pond of speakers.

I chose to claim the dress even if I was the only one wearing a gown.

I chose to claim my speech even though it was not the funny, casual type the other speakers had.

There's a reason I had 200 humans in the flesh, hundreds of tears, and a full room standing ovation!

This isn't by chance.

I have been preparing my nervous system for this moment.

It's easy to desire to speak on stage, but it's another to actively prepare your nervous system to be the version of you that can receive lots of attention, the fun kind, and the kind that makes you wish you could hide in the corner.

Confidence doesn't come from people recognizing you. It comes from you being able to recognize yourself.

The reason why so many coaches and creators feel behind, or less than on social media is because your body has unprocessed shame about your journey, your story, and your achievements.

To embody confidence is to expand your body's capacity to hold self-recognition, pride, and acknowledgment.

Only you can give that to yourself, not hundreds of likes or even thousands of followers.

Many people shy away from sharing their stories because it doesn't feel glamorous or anything special. Trust me, it's a whole lot more interesting and impactful than ten ways to calm your nervous system.

Imagine how different that post would be if it said, 'This is how I went from eating fast food while watching Netflix to actually knowing what foods energize my body and look ten years younger.'

It speaks to you because it's real; you can connect.

People are more likely to invest in someone who makes them feel, over someone who just teaches.

To practice this and embody self-recognition, I want you to boast about yourself. What have you achieved? What makes you an expert? What makes you special? What makes you unique?

Societal conditioning will have you believe that this bragging, I like to call this, remembering who the heck you really are.

Empowerment

How can you expect to create a community of powerful women if you focus on speaking to their pain and not their power?

This was the biggest mistake that I was making for such a long time because the marketing experts always taught that pain points are the only way to open pockets.

But it never felt right; it never felt fun or activating.

If you want to create content that actually helps and serves your audience in a deeper way, try this instead.

Plant seeds of hope in your content.

Empower your audience by speaking to who they inherently are, not just what their life circumstances might be at that moment.

What happens is instead of scrolling past another piece of content that makes them feel less than or keeps them in victim mode, your audience begins to feel activated, something sparks within, and they feel connected, they feel part of something bigger, they feel powerful.

And to be honest, it is so much easier for your audience to say yes to themselves and yes to working with you, coming from a space of empowerment rather than pain.

When you truly see your audience as resilient, passionate, creative, headstrong, empathic, present, and creative, there is a much lower chance you're going to feel the need to convince them or impress them.

Humanize the social media experience not just for yourself but for those who consume what you create.

Viral

The secret to going viral is to be okay with being the virus itself.

Everyone wants to create authentic content and fit into the algorithm, but you can't go viral if you're so terrified of being the virus yourself.

Being the virus is uncomfortable. People are quick to judge and blame; they have opinions about you. In order to hold that, your body needs to have the capacity to hold judgment, to hold fear, to hold projections.

Being the virus means having ideas, art, and beliefs that aren't the norm. They don't fit in the box of making everyone happy and only spreading good vibes.

If you are afraid of being seen, no hack or strategy, or even consistency will make you go viral.

If your body is protecting you from judgment, it's also protecting itself from authentic self-expression.

Start by sharing one polarizing truth, one thing you profoundly care about that feels like it pushes your edges of comfort, and practice getting uncomfortable so you can stretch your body's capacity to be seen by millions.

Judgment means you care. It's time to care MORE about impact than about what people will think.

Comparing

I f you're anything like me, you struggle big time with comparing yourself. I'm going to give you a little reframe that changed my life.

It's normal to compare yourself; it's a very real human experience.

So many people tell us to stop comparing ourselves, that it's wrong and unhealthy, but we all know what happens when we suppress, when we try to stop doing something — it doesn't go away, and in fact, it gets even louder.

Comparison isn't the enemy; it's the map of what is actually possible for you.

Comparison can either make you feel less than or jealous, and stop you from taking action.

Or, it can make you feel motivated and activated and ignited into action.

You don't have to stop comparing yourself. You just have to have the tools to channel it into truly experiencing self-acceptance in your body.

Next time you scroll on social media, and it seems like everyone is ten steps ahead of you, don't push that feeling away. There is a purpose there, a message, a powerful indicator of how you can step into the next level of accepting your true self.

Take a moment to go into your body. How does it make you feel? Explore this emotion, whether it's jealousy or anger or frustration.

Then ask your comparison as it lives in your body, what it needs from you today, what it desires, and how you can support it and express it, rather than suppress it.

Comparison can burn you to the ground or light your soul on fire.

The fire itself isn't bad. You just have to have the tools to stop burning yourself and instead ignite the fire into fuel and passion within to truly accept and celebrate how incredible you are.

Commitment

It's two weeks before my wedding, and I am fantasizing about my future husband cheating on me.

Most brides are dreaming up their flower arrangement, and my body is trying to escape the fear of commitment by imagining horrible things and getting myself so worked up.

My nervous system is a wreck. It's so ready to flee, searching for an escape card, running after a fantasy of no responsibility, no constraints.

Commitment feels like chains tying me down.

I used to think that freedom meant doing what I wanted, when I wanted. I used to think it meant I was accountable or responsible to no one.

But this type of freedom led me to run away from feeling anytime something became serious, long-term, forever.

I had to choose.

Free of feeling, or freedom to feel.

I spent much of my 20s imagining the most incredible business ideas. A fashion blog, a second-hand vintage store, a dance travel tour company, an international performer, a dance influencer, a social media agency for dancers, a YouTuber, a dance documentary, a marketing manager.

I didn't know what my own taste in music was, I didn't know what I wanted in a guy let alone a relationship, I didn't know what I felt like eating or what food I liked, I had no idea what my own style of clothing was.

I would sing whatever Top 40 music played on the radio, wear whatever was on sale at Zara, be with whatever guy gave me attention, and eat whatever food was cheapest on the menu.

I thought I was so free because I could choose anything, but I was chained by indecision, unfinished projects, and meaningless relationships.

There is instant gratification freedom when your actions are only motivated by the results you see today.

Then, there is long-term freedom when your actions are fueled by something bigger than today.

When we started dating, I told Kfir about my business ideas and that I was hesitating on buying a course to help me get started because I had a track record of having incredible ideas but never seeing them through to fruition.

He asked me one question that changed my life.

He asked, "Will you give up?"

I said, "No."

He said, "So it doesn't matter what the investment is; you're in it for the long run. Either way, you'll be successful."

Kfir is a forever person.

Kfir is my forever person.

I became free on my wedding day.

I became free when I chose forever.

Freedom is commitment

True freedom in relationships and in business isn't about living without constraints; it's about the capacity to devote to it for the long term.

Your capacity to stay the course, fueled by your long-term vision, is what separates you from being just another coach on the internet.

Whether in a relationship or in business, when there is still the safety card of 'it's not too late to back out,' the body does not have the capacity to receive deep intimacy and connection — meaning fast, quick, in-and-out type clients.

When your nervous system is flighty, subconsciously ready for an escape card, a fantasy of no responsibility, you tend to attract a one-night-stand type of client. Magic pill, quick win, hi and bye, no depth or loyalty.

I liberated the maiden identity of no responsibility and deeply devoted myself to the bigger long-term mission of a woman who can lead a movement and create a legacy.

I put my skin in the game, invested in long-term mentorship, and transformed my business into a devotion — not just something I do when I'm in the mood or feeling inspired.

Real freedom is the luxury of a grounded nervous system, and the capacity to deeply receive with ease through commitment and devotion for the long term.

True freedom is the capacity to make powerful choices and not have other people or situations make the choices for you.

Indecision is a sign the body doesn't feel worthy of personal power or trusting itself.

Commitment to yourself can only happen when your body feels worthy of how powerful it really is.

Making this shift on a body level happens when you make a scary commitment that feels uncomfortable, like it's stretching but, at the same time, specific and time-bound.

Just like a marriage contract or buying a house, you sign a contract, set agreements, and put money or a guarantee down, so too for your body.

This is where investments or a form of accountability will help to break this pattern by training and expanding your body's capacity to commit.

You don't have commitment issues, but you might have unprocessed indecisiveness blocked in your body.

In order to train your commitment muscle and keep your promises to yourself, the first step is to go to the core. This often comes from perfectionism and fearing shame or regret for making the wrong choices.

Most people try to force commitments like going 100% in business or quitting scrolling online. But the problem is, you can't force your body to change, you can't stop an old habit.

The real solution is to expand your body's capacity to process shame and regret. When your body can feel and liberate these emotions, instead of being pulled down, it can actually be channeled into boundaries and self-accountability.

For example, if you promised yourself that you would be consistent in your business, but you have a lot of shame that you have tried so many times in the past, and this is no different. Instead of forcing yourself to show up every day and dragging yourself into burnout, you do a somatic liberation practice and listen to what the body really has to say.

From there, you get to channel this emotion into action, such as investing in mentorship, connecting to inner trust in your body, or reaching out to collaborations.

For the longest time, I felt that being in a relationship with my then-boyfriend, now husband, was enough, and a wedding was totally unnecessary.

We know how to be partners, we know how to communicate, and we have each other; why do we need to make our commitment a public affair?

Something profound shifted in my body at my wedding, and my life complexity changed when I integrated it into my business.

Marriage allowed me to truly embody commitment. It allowed me to commit to myself, to know I can keep my own promises to myself.

A couples counseling course wasn't going to transform my commitment issues; making a sacred vow surrounded by the people I loved most would.

You may have all the knowledge, the courses, and the programs, but it's your deeply rooted fear of commitment that stops you from really embodying your next level.

Fears live in the body and aren't 'fixed' or 'changed' with more information. They are liberated with commitment.

If you are ready to step into your next level, it's time to prioritize embodying commitment, beyond knowledge and information in your brain. Train your commitment muscle in your body by deciding you are worthy of making a difference and making so much money.

Making a decision will set you free.

Either it will free you from responsibility for the immense power and success you are here for.

Or it will create freedom with incredible success, possibilities, and impact.

Chaos

In my early 20s, I was living out of a backpack when most people my age were so worried about knowing what their future would be, what jobs they would get after university, which car they were buying...

I mean, how on earth could you be in your 20s and not have your entire life sorted out?

How embarrassing?

We are conditioned to carry so much shame if we don't have full clarity of our lives.

Living out of my backpack and not knowing what my next destination would be taught me the most powerful life lesson that helped me make five-figure months in my business.

You can't think or plan your way into clarity. It's an embodied state that strengthens the more comfortable you become with not knowing.

The people with the most clarity are the ones who play the most with uncertainty and risks.

Not the ones who always know exactly where they are going and the final destination.

Like every emotion, feeling clear is a spectrum, and the more your body can experience confusion the more it can experience clarity.

Certainty comes from self-trust, a muscle practiced when you make decisions in the state of unknowing.

It's time to stop spending your time beating yourself up for not having clarity on your message, your purpose, or your identity, and instead, play in the realm of confusion and embrace the discomfort of uncertainty.

Celebrate the state of not knowing and a compass to your unique voice and pathway.

The truth is, you don't need clarity, you don't need to know your message fully, you don't need a website, and dare I say, you don't need certifications.

The only way to clarity is chaos.

The chaos of experimentation with your message, the chaos of so many ideas, the chaos of making time to prioritize posting.

The chaos of your mind saying, *this will never work*, and your heart saying it's the only way.

Most people wait until they're clear, aligned, and authentic to show up confidently on social media, but the only way to clarity is through taking action and showing up through the chaos and the unknown.

Clarity isn't a lack of certainty; it's your capacity to embrace the fear of not knowing and still maintain your commitment to what your intuition guided you to.

You can't think or plan your way into clarity; it's an embodied state that strengthens the more comfortable you become with not knowing.

The people with the most clarity are the people who play the most with uncertainty, with risks, with not knowing. Like every emotion, feeling clear is a spectrum, and the more your body can experience confusion the more it can experience clarity.

Certainly comes from self-trust, a muscle practiced when you make decisions in the state of unknowing.

Play in the realm of confusion, embrace the discomfort of uncertainty, and celebrate the state of not knowing.

Overthinking

S pending hours trying to find the best words for your sales copy is actually selfish.

If it's all about you, you'll be rewording your sales page and brainstorming your next offer for another six months.

If it's all about impact, you'll constantly go live to pour into your community and sell your offers every single day.

If your mission is to create powerful spaces for women who you know will change the world, this is not the time nor place to find yourself yet again overthinking how to articulate your message. It's selfish to let your fear, shame, or confusion get in the way of creating invitations for the impact your offers can have.

I'm just going to say it — it's actually selfish to spend hours and hours trying to figure out the best words for your sales copy.

Selfishness isn't bad; there is a time and place for it.

But if your mission is to create powerful spaces for women who will change the world, this is not a time nor place to find yourself yet again, overthinking the words of how to articulate your message and express what becomes possible for your clients when they join your world.

It's selfish to let your fear of coming across as too much, or the shame of what people would say, or the confusion of not knowing the next step get in the way of sharing your message and creating the invitations for the impact your offers have.

Overthinking means that your nervous system is working overtime and uses all its resources to protect you from possible discomfort.

Your capacity to move through these emotions and beliefs in your body, and take action with fear is actually where impact happens. You don't have the right words yet because you're not having a conversation.

If you want to be able to use your voice, platform, and time in a way that impacts thousands,

Go on live.

Host a workshop.

Send a voice message on your broadcast channel.

Sell your offer on your story.

The articulation, clarity, and expression come through in the act of SPEAKING!

Engagement earned.

You don't just deserve to have your offers fill up with the most embodied women just because you're an incredible coach.

You earn an overflowing business that feels so grounded in your nervous system by devoting yourself to your audience through sharing your voice and selling your offers

every

single

day.

Story Practice

Now is the fun part. Let's bring all the gold from this chapter into the most expressed, magnetic creator version of you to life!

1. Begin by noticing the discomfort that is present in your body when it comes to sharing your voice, being known, and unapologetically expressing yourself.

2. Bring it through the layers of the body: breath, posture, sensation, movement, shape, and space.

3. What does it want to say? What key phrase comes out of this character's throat?

4. Give that emotion or belief the microphone.

	Character A
Body	
Key Phrase	
What does it really want?	
How are you going to give this character a voice today?	

Part III: Service

Expand Your Capacity to Receive Massive Wealth

What is Wealth?

Money doesn't change the world — women who are a portal of wealth do.

All eyes are looking at me, and I wished the earth would swallow me up.

I had a measly $100 cash stuffed in a small zipper of my big orange backpack. I hadn't made the trip to the ATM in a few weeks from the African village I was staying at, and I was budgeting the last bits of cash for food for the upcoming weeks.

We are sitting on a cold cement floor, the only form of AC in town. There is a small gas fire on the floor cooking dinner and a big wooden grinder that we had just used to make some fresh peanut butter. While staying in the most beautiful small village in Malawi, this family had opened their home to me and showed me so much love and hospitality.

And today, the family is discussing the fees for the private school they want to send their daughter to.

I feel so embarrassed. I came to Africa on a one-way ticket to volunteer and to feel like I would make a difference, but I didn't have a spare $500 to help out with tuition after this family had opened their home to me.

What would taking pictures of schools for marketing fundraising do for the actual education of the kids of this village? Was I there just for my own little ego to feel I did something important, or could I actually make a bigger difference if I had money and resources to give?

For ten years, I dedicated myself to volunteering, hoping that I could change the world by donating my time.

I worked with special needs kids in Australia and children with cancer in the United States. I volunteered in hospitals in Israel and traveled around Africa for nine months, providing support in schools and women's centers.

I learned an important lesson that day: Giving my time doesn't make long-lasting change, money does.

In that moment, I let go of the naive story that I could save the world one volunteer job at a time, and realized I could create so much more impact when I made more money.

Almost a decade has passed, yet I see this belief system over and over with my clients.

I am so lucky to work with the most incredible, talented, wise women committed to making a difference, and it's often in these spiritual, heart-centered, deeply caring women who carry the most unfortunate and naive stories around money.

I hear things like:

- It's not about the money.

- Why is she sharing that she makes so much? That's devilish. Just keep it to yourself.

- I just want to help people. I don't care about how much I make.

I know these stories well because for a long time, I wore this mask of conditioning, which was actually for a deeper issue.

Disgust. Shame. Guilt.

On a deep body level, many spiritual coaches, embodiment mentors, and healers hold resentment and conditioning around money.

This is not actually about money itself; it's about the judgment or fear of what you will become with so much wealth.

We know that money amplifies who you are already, and is a tool for powerful change.

But this knowledge lives in the logical mind.

The body stores the deep disgust and conditioned beliefs, creating glass ceilings around wealth and long-lasting impact.

If you are ready to create revolutionary change in the world, the most powerful step is to look at the belief systems you have around wealth blocked in your body.

You can either continue being like the volunteer, giving all your time to create change, or you can be the one with resources, freedom, and power to create long-term change.

This is the chapter for wildly wealthy women who are ready to own their power of being able to create long-term change.

The ones who can buy land, live in nature, create homesteads, build retreat centers, create incredible work opportunities for others, give resources to schools, community centers, and charities, and spoil their loved ones.

The most present, liberated, wild woman is the one who can create generational wealth so that she can be present with herself and her loved ones and create a long-lasting, powerful impact without giving away all her time to create the change she wants to see in the world.

Saying Goodbye

"There's no heartbeat."

Mine or the thing inside me?

"Is there a husband or partner you want to call?"

Do I tell the polite, Christian pro-life nurse where I am getting a free ultrasound, that I've never been with someone longer than a month because as soon as there's attachment or feeling, I'm out?

"Your next step is to schedule a procedure at the hospital."

That's not even an option. I have a few dollars to my name. I just lost my dream job, and I have no more online freelancing clients after the world shut down. My country, where I have health benefits, closed the border, and I can't get in.

I drive back to the shared apartment. I start thinking, Where the heck did I go wrong? I feel delirious, too numb to feel anything. I thought I nailed the whole freedom lifestyle thing. I filled up a whole passport of stamps: six years to 35 countries.

Solo dancing world traveler.

Me, myself, and I.

Capital I.

The bigger the I, the less I would have to feel.

I go by myself, so I don't need to feel the pain of being left out.

I leave before I feel close, so I don't need to feel the pain of saying goodbye.

My body is gifting me the power to say goodbye.

Bye to habits that block out any intimacy.

Bye to a lifestyle that only has space for surface relationships.

Bye to the wounded maiden archetype, so there is capacity for depth, connection, and devotion.

***

You're only limited by that which you don't allow yourself to feel.

Massively growing your global movement and serving thousands of people to join your offers does not feel "safe, cozy, or comfortable in your body."

A lot of the time, it feels like saying a thousand goodbyes to past versions of yourself, past habits, friends, and comforts.

It's not about feeling good; it's about getting really good at feeling.

The deeper you can feel your grief, the more capacity you have to sell with conviction because you choose to care more about your clients' results than caring that you might piss some people off in the process.

The deeper you can feel your disappointment, the more capacity you have to do something with that frustration and shake up the world with the fiery offers that you know will change thousands of lives.

Selling isn't about avoiding discomfort; it's about prioritizing your clients' transformations over your own fears.

You can have all the nervous system trainings in the world, but if your body panics or freezes when you are upleveling, it's not a sign to calm down your nervous system. It's a cry for the fire within to turn into brave expression, taking up even more space and selling bigger than ever.

Distraction

I knew I was meant for something special — to have work that was so fulfilling I could feel it in my bones — but I didn't know exactly how, so I was busy with long to-do lists, my attention scattered with a million ideas...

Underneath distraction is what you wholeheartedly stand for.

Distraction is simply scattered focus.
Focus is warrior work.

This focus is direct; it knows what it deserves. It's fierce. It will fight for its beliefs no matter what.

Embody this warrior. What vision are you fighting for, and can you channel that energy of distraction into the energy of precision?

Distraction is asking you to make a decision, any decision, big or small, but make it with a fierce sense of self-knowing and focus.

You know when you feel like you're so close you can feel it, but just not quite there yet, the last step is believing it in your body.

It's great to know in your mind that you are powerful and confident, but if your body doesn't actually believe it, your body will stay in distraction or busy mode.

So the question becomes: How do you embody what you already know?

Everyone knows that if you exercise, you'll sleep better, have more energy, and gain muscle.

Not many people take their bums to the gym, and for those that do, how many commit to the daily commitment once the excitement wears off?

One week, two months, one year. Embodying what you know isn't about knowing how the machines work in the gym; it's the wear and tear of those muscles as a daily practice.

For example, you know that you are confident, but you've got to take that confidence to the gym daily.

Some days, it's the action of going live; some days, it's the action of sharing your message despite backlash. Sometimes it's changing your body language behind the scenes of you sharing your powerful work.

Unapologetic confidence doesn't happen from a journal prompt or meditation class. It happens when beliefs shift in your body.

Beliefs live in your body. All the mindset and energy work will only take you to a certain point.

Your capacity to make the impact you know will change the world doesn't happen by working harder in your business, putting in more hours, or by becoming more visible.

It happens when you break through belief systems protecting you from your next level.

When you are ready to penetrate, to get to the core, to shift beliefs on a core level requires somatics to shift.

This is the difference between dog paddling and swimming.

It takes more energy to paddle than it takes to create strong swim strokes, but the distance is incomparable.

Continuing your business with your current wealth glass ceiling ensures you will continue paddling. This will keep you in the pattern of always being busy working hard in your business.

You can either paddle or swim. Both are challenging and require commitment and energy.

The change happens when you decide to change your body, from small paddling movements near your chest to strong, long movements out towards the direction you are moving.

It's a lot more comfortable to paddle, and many coaches paddle for years.

But you're not like most coaches. You make the choice to join the swimming team and get around others who are taking massive leaps and movements to go way further distances.

> *Take a moment and fill your belly with a full breath.*
>
> *Sit up straight, open up your chest, and take a deep exhale from your stomach.*
>
> *What are all the directions the distraction is pulling you towards?*
>
> *Where is this pull the loudest in your body?*
>
> *Does it feel like fire? Is it tight? Urgent?*
>
> *Create a shift in posture, and open spaciousness in your heart.*
>
> *Access the courage to give yourself what your body is really asking for.*
>
> *What is the voice of this focus? What does it want to say?*
>
> *Take this laser beam and create from this space today.*

Rejection

I have never stood out like a sore thumb more than at this moment.

I catch a glimpse of myself in the studio mirror. I am surrounded by petite dancers in leotards, slick back hair, and ballet shoes.

I am wearing a white crop top, baggy purple sweatpants, and clunky white sneakers (they were trendy at the time). My curly hair is all frizzy from running to catch the tram to arrive on time.

It's a massive day of auditions, and I had it set in my heart since I arrived back home from Africa that dance was my future and I would find my way to perform on massive stages.

I didn't think about it before, but everyone in the room is younger than me and has probably been in dance classes since they were 4. I have never taken dance classes, but I have danced at nightclubs and spent the last nine months dancing in villages in Africa, feeling so alive with the music, culture, and rhythm, so that is something.

But as I listen to the instructions for the audition that sound like they are in another language, I start deciding whether I should leave before I make a fool of myself.

This isn't freestyle, this is a routine, a standard, an industry in which

I do not fit at all.

I take a deep breath and choose to stay and give it my all.

My number is not called at the end.

I turn to the girl next to me. She looks extremely disappointed, and she politely smiles and says, "I guess I'll see you at the next one."

Oh no you won't, I think, but I smile back.

I don't see rejection as an excuse to wait. I see rejection as an opportunity to create my own path there.

I believed I was going to perform on stages in front of thousands of people with no dance background.

Everyone thought I was delusional.

The truth is, I was delusional. No one in their right mind believes that much in themselves that they are willing to endure so much embarrassment, rejection, failure, and judgment.

Belief is delusional because you need to embody this version of you before there is proof or results.

"I'll believe it when I see it" is not actually belief, it's wishful thinking and keeps you waiting, wishing, dreaming, fantasizing, and in your mind.

But I don't live in my mind; I live in my body, so when I got rejected at the audition, instead of waiting for the next audition date like all the other dancers in the room, I created my own pathway to getting on stage.

"I believe it, so I create it" is how belief works.

I surrounded myself with videographers, networked with brands, and I created an opportunity where a week later, I was performing a dance segment on national television. Within a couple of weeks, I was on a plane to be a part of the dance team in the Dominican Republic.

All the other dancers in the audition waited for the next audition date and let time choose for them.

Through belief work and embodiment, I jumped timelines instead.

I was not the best dancer. I was the best at believing in myself.

This belief work is exactly how I have grown a multi-six-figure movement that impacts thousands.

"Your dreams don't create a global movement, your beliefs do."

If your body doesn't believe the words you say in the mirror, writing I am a millionaire ten times every day in your journal or the beautiful vision board you stuck above your desk won't actually work.

Beliefs live in your body and transform on a cellular level, not a mind level.

Let's try it together:

> *The way we create long-lasting change is first to realize that your body's wisdom is giving you exactly what you desire all the time.*
>
> *In order to shift your beliefs on a body level, the first step is to see how not having this desire is actually serving you. What is the emotion or sensation you get from not having the thing?*
>
> *Underneath, there is usually a sense of comfort, joy, coziness, love, acceptance, belonging, and relaxation. Your nervous system doesn't know the difference between joy from making less money and having fewer responsibilities from the joy that comes from recurring income and more options.*
>
> *Now, the second step is crucial: Create a radical new possibility for experiencing that same sensation in an entirely different way.*

Fill your day with these actions that embody this new belief on an emotional and sensational level rather than mechanically repeating affirmations. Let your body rewrite the codes to actually be able to believe in the change you are calling in.

Overwhelm/Chaos

O verwhelm is your body preparing for abundance.

Overwhelm isn't a sign you're doing too much. It's a sign you're thinking too much.

Overwhelm means there is so much in your system, and your nervous system is screaming to stop. It's so much to feel. You know what else is so much? Overflow.

It doesn't fit into the cup, and it tips over and splashes everywhere.

Overwhelm and overflow are two sides of the same coin.

If this powerful energy of *so much* gets stuck in your mind, it's labeled as overwhelm, and when it moves through your body, it's called overflow.

If you allow yourself to feel *so muchness,* you are training your nervous system to be able to receive an overflowing amount of wealth, joy, and success.

So the next time Miss Overflow visits, turn on some music, let her take up every inch of your body, and then take that fiery energy into one edgy, brave, radical action.

Overwhelm is all about you, so it stays stuck in the mind and turns into a headache, second-guessing, or snapping at someone.

Overflow is about the collective, so it moves through the body and turns into invitations, expressions, and connections. Either way, you will experience so much, the choice is: Which one are you choosing today?

When your nervous system is experiencing overwhelm, it's protecting you from chaos. But guess what also has a lot of chaotic energy? *Abundance.*

Your nervous system doesn't know the difference between overwhelm and abundance; they are both experienced as so much in your body.

Imagine the sensation of your phone buzzing with PayPal notifications, new clients onboarding, people referring, and DMs asking you how to join your program.

If your body is used to dissociating when there's chaos, it will cockblock all your success as a form of protection.

When your body blocks so muchness of overwhelm, it's also blocking your capacity to receive so much money.

This is muscle strengthening for success in your body.

If you leave the weight on your body, you'll get bruises.

If you lift the weights daily, you'll get results.

The weight is the same in both scenarios. Your choice and capacity to lift it is where the results happen.

So next time you're experiencing overwhelm in your business, with your ideas, thoughts, or to-do lists, remember that the more capacity your body has to experience overwhelm, the more capacity it has to experience so much of the things you desire.

Disgust

Her face grimaced.

It was so slight, but across the Zoom room, oceans apart, I knew we had just struck gold.

At 2pm, the most dreamy client sent me a DM saying that she was ready to earn her living fully from her medicine, and she felt that the piece that was missing lies in her body.

By 6pm, she was in for six months of mentorship.

I could tell by our conversation in the DMs that she was ready. She was all in, and she was looking for embodied mentorship that went to the core of patterns and beliefs in her body.

I'll never forget our 1:1 somatic session; I knew history was made that day. We came face-to-face with a powerful block that was living in the body.

Disgust.

Disgust for charging.

Disgust for only business coaches making all the wealth.

Disgust around money, years worth of stories, and conditioning that medicine women shouldn't get paid, or are expected to do healing work for free.

Disgust was showing up as a belief that her medicine was not valuable enough to charge a lot of money for.

Even though she knew her work was life-changing, her body was carrying disgust that was blocking her from being known, from being magnetic, and from having overflow with clients who were so excited to pay her.

Through a powerful *Body Talk* practice for disgust, she was able to physically purge this long-held belief in her body. That same day, she went all in on her social media and fully showed up as the version of herself who owned her medicine. The whole world could hear and feel her, and within a few months, she was having her first $20,000 month as a medicine woman, facilitating powerful shamanic work.

The more you value your time, skills, gifts, and medicine, the more you share.

The more you share your message with conviction and excitement, the more you become known and the more people you get to reach.

The more people you reach, the more trust builds for your offers.

The more trust people have in your work, the easier it is for people to say yes to themselves and pay you to guide them.

The easier it is for people to say yes to themselves, the more your medicine creates change in the world.

You can facilitate the most powerful medicine in the world. Still, without your body deeply believing in its value and mastering the art of communicating your message effectively, it may not reach and impact the lives it has the potential to change.

Your gifts are too important to be hidden behind resistance, fear, excuses, and discomfort.

If selling makes you feel gross, then this is about to make you a lot of sales.

You don't have a money problem. You have surpassed shame in your body.

Money is neutral — it's your relationship with receiving it that is impacting your ability to sell in a way that feels fun and aligned.

The emotion of disgust is so common when it comes to money and selling, so let's look closer because your body is giving you the key to so much wealth.

Any time your body is giving you a signal like an emotional reaction, a mental reaction, or a physical reaction, it means it's trying to tell you something really important.

> *Drop into your body for a moment and connect to the sensation of disgust. Your nostrils might flare, there might be a wrenching in your gut, nausea in your stomach.*
>
> *The natural result of eating rotten food is that your body experiences the need to throw up, to clean itself of something harming your system.*
>
> *When you experience disgust when it comes to selling, your body is trying to throw up ideas and beliefs that are not serving your greater good.*
>
> *Remember, beliefs live in the body, so purging an old belief doesn't happen in some magical mindset practice; it is experienced in the body through a somatic liberation practice.*
>
> *If you feel gross when it comes time to sell your incredible offer, this is a sign you are ready to somatically cleanse yourself of an old belief that has been holding you back.*
>
> *What belief is it time to let go of? What are you holding on to that isn't actually yours or serving you?*

Letting go of this belief happens in actively selling with pleasure. This is the opposite of what your body wants, aka your conditioning.

What is one way you can connect to pleasure in your system and invite your audience from that space?

Your clients need your offer, and you need to liberate disgust in your body so you can share it in a way that makes them feel a full-body yes to join.

Martyr

"I don't want a present this year," I said proudly.

I feel like I am an angel sent to save my family from financial struggles.

I'm in the shopping mall with my siblings.

The AC is full blast, and we are in the toy section. We have been waiting for this day all year. Every year on the Jewish holiday, Hanukkah, my family had a tradition that we got to choose price points that were our age.

This year, I was 9 years old, but I wasn't scanning the isles looking for anything that was $9.

I had already decided there would be no present for me this year. I had overheard that my father's business had declared bankruptcy, and I didn't want to burden him with my present.

I look at my father, surrounded by a bunch of my siblings, all excited with the toy they had chosen.

I searched for my father's face. I see his hair starting to turn white, wrinkles underneath his glasses, and his tired, soft mouth.

I stood a little taller. I felt so big. I felt I was saving my father the stress of $9. I felt so important and proud — a huge badge of honor.

I'm not a little kid who needs toys. I am saving the world by not causing my family extra pain or stress.

I learned at a young age that I was here to make a difference and support others, which meant carrying the weight of the world.

- Giving up my Hanukkah gift at age 9 to save money for the family

- Wearing hand-me-downs to carry the burdens so I was not one

- Working as a babysitter to be independent

It all made me feel like I was making a change.

I felt so proud to carry this badge of honor.

That I was doing God's work.

***

For years, I lived my life with this silent belief that carrying money burdens or even carrying anyone's burden is honorable.

This showed up when I was trying to scale my business and kept hitting a glass ceiling.

My nervous system is attached to the identity of carrying the weight of the world, being a one-woman show, being perfect, never disappointing anyone or the belief no one can do it better than anyone else than myself.

I was glued to my work and refused to hire any assistance in something I could easily do.

When your body has an attachment to the identity of being a one-woman show, it's known as somatic martyrdom, receiving a sense of pride or recognition from overworking or sacrificing physical and mental well-being for the sake of others or their responsibilities.

This isn't transformed in a business training or some strategy to manage your team. This is transformed in the body because this is a core pattern that is often generational or passed down.

The first step is to become aware of how this identity is gaining or benefiting, what they receive from being in this pattern.

Pride, acknowledgment, recognition.

To shift this at a body level, we want to transform that fuel. For example, pride can be transformed into leadership, into creativity, into trust for your team.

This transformation isn't just about shifting behaviors; it's about reclaiming your power and unlocking your full potential.

By recognizing the sources of pride and acknowledgment tied to being a 'one-woman show,' and by redirecting that energy into leadership, creativity, and trust in your team, you're not just changing your approach to work — you're redefining what success means for you.

Once I shifted this, hired my first team member, and stopped helicoptering my clients — my income tripled, and I felt more alive and joyful than ever.

I'm learning one of the most spiritual things I can do is make a lot of money and become a conduit of change.

No more carrying the weight of the world.

It's not my job anyhow.

That's God's work...and I think he handled it well.

Imposter Syndrome

My heart sinks.

"Here, take this skirt. I just went shopping, and I'm not going to wear this anymore."

Usually, I'd be so excited. I love going to her house because she's always buying new things and I get to get what doesn't fit in the closet anymore.

But not today.

Today, my father is here. He is downstairs in the study fundraising for our Jewish Community Center.

We have plans to go to my friend's holiday house on the ocean to spend the day on the jet ski and watch movies in the living room while the golden light sunset from the ocean pours in.

Yet, while I'm having fun, my father asks my friend's father for money.

And for the first time, I feel uncomfortable receiving these small favors from my friend.

I squint. I feel a bit sick to my stomach.

I suddenly feel sorry for myself that I don't have a holiday house like my friend and that receiving from her makes me feel like a pity case.

***

When there is shame around receiving, the body is blocking abundance.

Whether it's a favor, a compliment, or a loan, if the nervous system associates receiving to being a charity, being needy, or not being good enough, it stops the flow coming to you.

I know all the coaches online are trying to convince you that imposter syndrome is something you need to fix, but in reality, it's your selling superpower.

Let me explain.

Imposter syndrome is your body communicating that it feels inadequate to promote your work because it doesn't feel deserving of receiving.

Basically, you feel embarrassed to sell your coaching offer because you don't feel you are the fully healed, fully perfect, fully successful version who deserves to accept a lot of money in exchange for your offers.

Imposter syndrome is simply suppressed shame living in your body.

If it's unprocessed, it turns into avoiding responding to messages or underselling your offers.

When shame is liberated in the body, it turns into full-body magnetic selling because your audience feels so connected, so empowered, and so activated by your message.

Any time imposter syndrome comes to visit, which is especially loud when you're launching and promoting yourself, it's a reminder to embody what you teach and give your own tools to yourself.

People want to buy from real humans; they want to buy an embodied transformation, not just a perfect end result.

A health coach authentically sells because they have struggled with weight themselves, so they deeply relate to their client's fears and concerns.

A spiritual coach authentically sells because they have struggled with darkness and can hold compassion and relatability for their clients.

You don't have to fix your imposter syndrome. You just have to associate receiving with power versus victim.

Remember, a powerful leader is someone who goes out to the battlefield with their army. Even when they are scared, they lead with fear.

Selfish

"At least you're not selling something at the end."

I was shocked.

It was the first time a video of mine went viral, reaching over one million people.

Over 80,000 real humans took the time to like this video, and over a thousand people moved their fingers and wrote comments.

Many of those comments were deeply thanking me for this message and most of the comments asked how they could deepen their embodiment practice to stop getting so lost in their minds.

Over a thousand people asked what the next step was.

But this one comment celebrating the fact that I didn't "sell" was what caught my attention.

There were thousands of people left empty-handed because of my fear of these types of comments, but truly, from this belief system, if you give value, it should be free.

Not selling is actually the most selfish thing you can do.

Picture this: You are at a stadium with thousands of people, and you share your story of how you overcame the hardest mental and emotional period of your life through various twenty-minute embodiment practices that you could easily share with them.

But because it might come across as salesy or annoying, you keep your mouth shut.

Selling is not the devil. Selling yourself short is.

If you truly believed in the value of your work and the life-changing transformation it provides, you would be selling all the time.

You don't have a money mindset problem, you have beliefs in your body about the value of your methodology.

You believe you are worthy of growth, so you invest thousands in trainings, certifications, coaching, healing, masterminds, etc.

Your body fully backs these decisions because you are confident it's going to transform your life.

But when it comes to charging thousands for your own offers, all of a sudden, there is contraction and resistance, and your body feels small and less than. Fear takes over the driver's seat...

This isn't actually about money.

This is about your beliefs about your own value.

There are many types of generosity — some societies consider it selfless and others selfish.

It's easy to see someone volunteering at a soup kitchen as selfless, and in the same breath, it's easy to conclude that a person who has their face plastered on billboards promoting their brand is selfish.

What you don't see is what that person is funding is actually the soup kitchen...

It's easy to see your work as so admirable that you help so many people, but in the same breath, you are judging yourself for celebrating a milestone and worried you would come across as distasteful while people are suffering.

Generosity is selfless.

The journey to generosity can be viewed as selfish.

Can you hold the paradox in your body?

When I celebrate a massive milestone in my business, a big part wants to push it under the rug because of the fear of people thinking I'm full of it.

But celebrating my milestones is what has planted the seeds for so many that this is possible for them, which is the reason why I am able to help so many more people.

You are someone who deeply cares, but often your body can block your capacity for generosity because of coming across as selfish, arrogant, or egotistical.

The more you step into generosity — the more you stretch your capacity for coming across as selfish.

Money is a value exchange.

When you deeply believe your work changes the world, on a body level, your offers will become the investments your dream clients are praying for.

Your current beliefs equal the current amount in your bank account.

Are you ready to shift your beliefs?

Create proof that continuously reminds your body of how powerful and life-changing your offers are.

Some examples are:

- Give, give, give.

- Go on Instagram and facilitate the powerful work you do.

- Host a monthly workshop. Collect the data, collect the proof, and collect the connection and impact.

Share your story over and over again and how you gave yourself the tools that created this powerful transformation.

Each time you remind yourself of how YOU changed YOUR life, you build this confidence around the incredible value of your offers.

Celebrate in your body and to your community the wins that became possible through the offers you share.

Read over your testimonials as a devotion. Really see the lives that have been impacted and the ripple effect that has been created.

You can have the most transformative methodology in the world, but without your body deeply believing in its value and mastering the art of communicating your message effectively, it becomes harder to create the global impact you know you are here for.

Gratitude

The movers are bringing all the boxes and furniture into our new oceanfront apartment we just rented. It's a hot and sticky August day on the island. I stand outside on the porch to try to get out of their way, but I can't shake the nagging feeling inside.

This is everything I dreamed of. Why don't I feel grateful? I thought, as I looked over the Caribbean crystal clear blue waters.

I start every morning with three things I am grateful for, but there is a big difference between experiencing logical gratitude in the mind and embodying gratitude as a true felt sense in the body.

Consciously, I was so grateful, but my body had not caught up yet. My nervous system was so used to the comfort of less rent and fewer responsibilities it wanted to curl up into a ball and hide.

When I gave myself the space to feel, so much guilt came through.

You can write in your gratitude journal all day long, but if there is unprocessed guilt in your body, this gratitude only lives on a mind level, not a body level.

If you feel like you should be grateful, instead of forcing it because everyone says, *how dare you not,* get curious about what is actually present in your body.

For example, your brain says, *You should be grateful you got this amount of clients*, but your body is saying, You could have done better. The emotion of guilt is trying to express itself.

If you try to cover this guilt by planting on a smile and trying to feel grateful for what you already have, that's where silent resentment begins to build up.

When you listen to this guilt instead of ignoring it, you get to go to a deeper level of actually feeling deserving of your desires.

This will allow you to experience the feeling of gratitude in your body.

We live in a time where gratitude is so glorified as some secret weapon for getting your desires, but shaming yourself for not feeling grateful is counterintuitive.

If you want to truly embody a sense of gratitude that vibrates in every cell of your body and actually expands your nervous system capacity to receive more of the thing you are grateful for, whenever you hear the word *should next* to a feeling, pause.

Become aware of what emotion is trying to express itself and let yourself fully feel it.

Guilt

I'm sitting in the front seat with our dog, Callie, feeling sick to my stomach.

Kfir is driving me to the airport. This would be the first time we are apart for this long since we started dating.

I have my phone in hand, and I am booking my accommodation for the night I arrive before my ten-day somatic facilitator immersion begins in the jungle of Costa Rica.

It feels like forever since my backpacker days when I would just find the cheapest hostel and sleep on a bunk bed with a dozen strangers.

We are newly married, my business is just starting to pick up momentum, and what I really want is a comfortable bed, a beautiful view, and a desk with fast Wi-Fi as I have a session with my clients early morning before our four-hour ride to the retreat property.

Kfir encouraged me to book a beautiful hotel for the night, but I felt so guilty about staying alone in a five-star hotel — it felt excessive and unnecessary.

After going back and forth many times, I finally booked the hotel and as $300 left my account, my stomach flipped in a circle.

I did not grow up with materialistic luxury; I never stayed in a hotel or ate at restaurants as a kid.

I had this story in my mind that spending so much money on food and accommodation beyond necessity made you spoiled, which meant you would be unappreciative and disrespectful.

It's this love-hate relationship: *I want you, but I feel so guilty for wanting you.*

This guilt often comes from the language we grew up hearing about money.

"They're not actually fulfilled behind all that wealth."

"Money doesn't buy happiness."

"Too much money ruins families."

It doesn't matter if you read every money mindset book in the world.

You can't think your way out of money blocks; you can't logic your way into feeling deserving of more.

Guilt is a moral compass that protects belief systems that live in the body, such as fear of abandonment, being spoiled, or irresponsible.

This belief is beyond logic. Having a great income doesn't automatically make the body feel deserving.

Logically knowing you are worthy isn't going to overflow your bank with zeros.

I woke up in the morning and tried to feel excited by the mountain view, but all I could feel was my stomach doing backwards flips. *$300, you could have done so much more with your hard-earned money other than a view.*

I decided if my tummy wouldn't stop talking, I might as well fill it with the breakfast buffet, but as I sat down alone with all the flavored yogurts and assortment of pastries my mind said, *Just because you stay at a nice hotel, doesn't mean you get to stuff your face. Look, you're just turning into one of them.*

Enough.

I went back to my room.

I put on some music and decided to get to the bottom of what this guilt was trying to tell me.

Instead of logically convincing myself I was deserving of luxury, I explored what this repressed belief system in my body was really trying to say.

The emotion of guilt felt like it wanted to hide under the bed. It was small and embarrassed, and what it was really asking for was to feel appreciated and to feel spoiled.

My body was asking for permission to be spoiled. Yes, the thing it was terrified of, being perceived as being a spoiled brat, actually wanted to feel that sensation and didn't have the words to ask other than acrobats in my stomach, which felt like guilt and undeservingness.

So I spent the day experiencing self-appreciation and the sensation of spoiling myself through childlike glee and enjoyment, swimming in the pools and dancing around the beautiful property.

Transforming money beliefs does not happen in the mind; they are passed down in the body so if you want to feel worthy of so much more, explore money beliefs in the body and liberate what those beliefs and repressed emotions are asking from you.

Proud

My cheeks are burning, although it's a chilly Friday afternoon. I angrily open up the white van door and tell my friend to follow me. Food wrappers are on the floor; there is a funky smell and I sit next to the window and quickly open it up. This is the last time I'm inviting a friend to my house for the weekend, I promise to myself under my breath.

School finished more than half an hour ago, but I knew the Bentleigh Bus always runs late, so I tried stalling and taking our time, but we were still, as usual, the last to be picked up.

We stop on the way to do some errands, and I am secretly hoping my friend gets a stomach ache and we would drop her home before we drive all the way to my house.

After what feels like an eternity, we finally pull into our driveway, packed with fridges and boxes of fruit because that's the best place for storage obviously.

I tell my friend to follow me. I rush her through the house straight to my room. I practically ran up the stairs so she wouldn't catch any mess. I take the broken door handle off so my siblings wouldn't bother us and breathe a sigh of relief, mumbling under my breath that when I have my own home, I will never let my kids feel embarrassed to bring friends over.

***

Something falls from the tree above me. I look up and there are two boys laughing, throwing us some fruit they are picking.

"Gracias," I smile back at them as I peel the Caribbean fruit and pop it in my mouth.

"They're so excited to show you their home," the tour guide tells us.

We are visiting an indigenous village in the Costa Rican rainforest where the whole family sleeps in the same room on the floor.

"The Original Rich People," he says proudly, "They have what everyone is trying to find."

The tour guide continues as he takes us to the mother of the family.

She graciously shows us how to make homemade Cacao in her outdoor kitchen with a couple of utensils, a single wood burner, and two chairs. She laughs as my friend, and I struggle with the large stone used for grinding the beans.

I watch her kids play with their friends.

They look about the age that I was so embarrassed to invite friends to my house and all these years later, I finally learn what it means to be rich.

If you want to become rich, you have to become proud.

Being rich doesn't mean having the biggest house; being rich is a feeling of being able to be at home, within your body, within your relationships, and within your work.

These people are not ashamed of how they live. In fact, they invite people from all over the world to visit them.

Rich people are proud of what they have, no matter the amount.

They celebrate their wins and achievements loud and clear and put their names on plaques and charities for all to see.

We spend so much time trying to get rich, doing all the hard work, and staying in the rat race when we have blocked shame in the body.

If you want to focus on living a rich life, you have to be so proud of who you are and what you have accomplished each and every step of the way.

Procrastination

I'm sitting on a pillow in the corridor. It's after the Shabbat meal on Friday night. My two sisters and I have all created our little reading nook in the area of the house that still has the lights on.

I'm so excited because I picked up a new book from the library. It is a love story, and I'm just getting to the good part.

My stomach started doing little butterflies as the scene played out about a boy falling madly in love with a girl.

I closed my eyes and imagined my Prince Charming one day sweeping me off my feet and running off into forever together.

I took this fantasy with me into the big world of boys, and all I could think about was how it would feel to make someone fall in love with me.

My focus was: *How could I get more pleasure? How could I have more fun? How could I have a guy falling over his face for me?*

Capital ME!

After a few years, the butterflies in my stomach were getting tired from running to find this romanticized fairy tale I had hoped for.

I felt like I was running, but in the opposite direction of forever.

It took a massive wake-up call to learn what these butterflies really were saying.

It started with the shift from me, me, me, to you, you, you

Procrastination being stuck in the capital ME phase.

Short-term soothing versus long-term deepening.

We so easily get lost in a world of to-do lists, running in circles around goals or expectations that are exhausting us, not just physically, but somatically.

In reality, what's really happening is your body begging to feel alive, to feel the emotions that make us human.

Procrastination is an alarm clock for your soul — a remembering of what your soul really came onto this earth for — deep connection, creativity, expression, joy, fulfillment.

It makes sense that you are feeling overwhelmed by little tasks. Little talks are keeping you busy from feeling what you're actually scared to feel

The energy of procrastination is always running — either it's running in loops in your mind, keeping you stuck, or it's running towards what you deeply desire. You choose.

If you want to be in a forever type of relationship, you want the we to be louder than the me.

Business is a forever type of relationship.

You are creating a legacy, not a one-night stand.

It's not about getting clients, or getting more money.

But more about giving, and how you can add more value to the market.

Being good at business is not something you need a suit and tie for.

It's something you need a heart and soul for.

So next time you get intimidated by the business side of things, come back to your heart and ask yourself how you can be of service today.

Have you ever tried to do so many things at one time that nothing gets done?

You are trying to be productive and save time, but you're actually having to redo things because you are not actually present.

Here is what you can do instead of making another Google Calendar or to-do list.

Take one moment to breathe and feel. That's it.

Time management isn't a discipline issue; it's a nervous system issue.

If you struggle to manage your time, this is your reminder that you don't need to be more organized; you need to feel more.

If you don't know why you are procrastinating — why you leave things to the last minute even when you KNOW you shouldn't — just know this.

Procrastination is internal chaos that feels familiar. If there was chaos or inconsistency growing up, the chaos feels familiar to your body, to your nervous system.

So even though, as an adult, you know logically that constantly being distracted isn't helpful, your nervous system actually enjoys being in that chaos.

Your nervous system will always choose familiar suffering over unfamiliar success.

So, instead of shaming yourself or feeling guilty for wasting time, notice what this state is actually asking from you. What is it really asking for and give that moment to yourself.

A regulated nervous system is ten times more productive than an anxious one.

Your body is asking you to listen through feeling what you're running from.

There's nothing wrong with running itself; it's just a matter of which direction you are going.

Speed

When I was little, my mom told me that if you watch the numbers on the microwave while your food is inside, the time goes slower.

It's not the time that slows down; what slows down is your capacity to receive the results you are working on.

I used to stare at my income and social media metrics like it was my full-time job, and every time it went up, I felt amazing, but when it went down, it was like time stopped, and I would be sucked into a vacuum of inner criticism and comparison.

I spent so much time searching for peace in achievements, but it never seemed to be enough.

Another income goal, another follow, another vacation — I was achieving all my goals, but I still didn't feel the depth of what I was searching for.

On the outside, I made it — I achieved the dreams and goals that I set for myself, but on the inside, there was an emptiness that never felt enough.

Everything changed when I realized I had been looking for peace in all the wrong places.

Instead, I began to search for this peace within me and my body.

The funny part is, I didn't have to search, my body already knew this peace. It was just a matter of learning how to remember.

I started measuring success to the degree I felt present in my life.

Success as a felt sense rather than a badge of honor.

I stopped watching the numbers because I was too busy living an extraordinary life, but the numbers always grew because at the end of the day, numbers are only a by-product of how alive and embodied you are.

Entitled

There is no such thing as the right time.

99% of people are waiting for aligned timing but the 1% don't believe that the right time even exists. They know that the right time is only when they believe in themselves.

I don't think you will ever meet a wealthy woman who said her quantum leap happened exactly when she felt ready, and all the cards were in order.

Most breakthroughs, most transformations, often happen at the most inconvenient times, when everything is messy and confusing, and inside of that growth spurt is the birth, when resilience and self-worth go into full gear.

It's time to stop outsourcing your power to a coach, to something you saw on social media, to your schedule, the season, to astrology, or even to feeling ready.

Aligned timing happens the moment you decide to go all in.

When you feel entitled to take a chance on yourself, when you actually feel deserving of spending more time with your family, when you feel worthy of making more money, when you feel worthy of seeing yourself standing in front of women, feeling so confident about making a difference.

The only right time is this exact moment when you fully commit to feeling so entitled as a human being to make the most out of your time on this precious life on this earth.

Time can either feel like it's rushing you, or like the rush of living fully alive.

Time

Money doesn't buy happiness, but it does buy time.

And the more you buy back your time, the happier you become.

For a couple hundred dollars a month, I have a house manager who creates delicious home-cooked meals and cleans my home, so I can spend the afternoons at the ocean with my husband, which makes me so happy.

For a couple thousand dollars a month, I have a team to manage my business, and mentors help me fast-track my income so that I can focus on what I love most about my work, which is somatic mentorship with my clients and creating masterpieces with my self-expression, which also leaves me feeling overjoyed and fulfilled.

This is a snowball effect that just keeps growing, but where does it start?

The first step is to deeply value your time.

But not logically, because your mind knows all the things you should do just creates a never-ending to-do list that leads to stress, fear around time running out, rushing and burning out.

Deeply valuing your time only happens on a body level.

> *Take a full breath and exhale with me. Notice what your shoulders are carrying in this moment, any tension in your chest or numbness in your legs.*

In this moment of awareness, you get the experience of full-body aliveness, which only exists in the present moment.

Time doesn't live in the past of what you could have done, or in the future of what you should do.

Time only lives in this moment, and the only way to experience this actual moment is in your body.

So, if you're worried about repeating patterns, choose to repeat this one.

Value your time more by getting out of your head and into your body so you can be in a state of service, making you more income. With that money, invest in offers that buy you back your time so you can make even more, and then come back to valuing your time even more by raising your transformation and prices. Your happiness and fulfillment will continually grow.

Delusion

Call me delusional, but making a $20k+ cash week while on a romantic getaway becomes so normalized in your nervous system when we sell to the body. This way, your audience doesn't need to be in their logical minds and are able to be so genuinely excited to join your offers.

The truth is, it's so much easier for your nervous system to sell to the body than to sell to the logical mind, but no one actually teaches HOW…

157 changemakers have bought our mystery offer without knowing any details because of the *Selling to the Body Method*.

Right now, you're in your head when you're selling.

You're still thinking about the name, the price, the number of weeks, and in constant busy planning mode.

You're not yet the living, breathing 3D proof of the transformation of your offer, and your audience can feel it.

You're still asking your mentor to review your content when, in fact, *you're asking for permission to unleash your voice and say what most people are not saying on the internet.*

You're still screenshotting your favorite coach's story slides as the key to articulating your offer, *but forgetting the goosebumps they gave you goes beyond the words they use.*

You're still sticking to the strategy and the past ways of selling when *all you really want to do is sing, dance, hire a videographer, and produce a masterpiece.*

Your selling feels like every other coach on the internet, but if we were to be really honest, the sessions you facilitate are mind-blowing, unique, and irreplaceable!

Hundreds of your dream clients buy your mystery offer without any details because of the way you make them FEEL, and that begins with YOU getting really good at FEELING!

Scarcity

Scarcity is <u>wanting</u> more.

Abundance is giving more.

Instead of <u>wanting</u> more clients, become the person who shows up and over-delivers every single day, and watch your dream clients overflowing into your inbox.

Instead of <u>wanting</u> more money, embody the most wealthy version of yourself that knows she deserves it all, and with that knowledge, sell your services with so much excitement and love every single day. Money simply becomes a by-product.

Instead of wanting more followers, prioritize nourishing your creative muscle of self-expression every day because it brings you so much joy.

Most people spend their lives always wanting, wishing, and waiting, but the people who are actually experiencing success and freedom are slightly delusional.

They don't entertain questions like, "How is this even possible?" Or "It's not the right time."

Look around you, it's not the smartest people, it's not even the most disciplined or luckiest people that make the most money.

It's the person who is committed to creating more results and trans-formations for others.

> *Write a list of why you deserve to go all in, why you are entitled to take a chance on yourself, why you deserve to spend more time with your family, why you deserve to spoil your mom with luxury vacations, and why you specifically are worthy of making more money.*
>
> *Now spend five minutes every morning for the next week and fully commit to feeling this worthiness in your body, allowing the sensation to flow through you.*
>
> *Then each day, take one uncomfortable action that this version of you would take.*

Different

I want to tell you a story about a girl who was always different.

In primary school, I was the only religious kid, so whenever there were birthday parties I always had to bring my own food.

I made it my thing.

In high school I was different.

Most of my friends had holiday homes, and I worked as a babysitter, making my own money to spend whenever we went out.

I made it my thing.

After high school, everyone I knew was studying in seminary.

I volunteered in a hospital instead.

I made it my thing.

Then everyone my age was going to university, and I went to travel solo across the world.

I made it my thing.

At this point, my friends were all getting married, and I was performing on stage in front of thousands in the Caribbean.

I made it my thing.

When I started my business, all my entrepreneurial friends fit so neatly into their niche boxes while I embraced my multi-passionate self and launched whatever I felt like in that season.

I made it my thing.

Everyone says they want to make a difference, but how much capacity do you have to feel the pain of being different?

Doing something different is the hard part because we are designed to want to fit in.

In order to make a difference, we have to train the muscle of being different.

What do you want to say that no one is saying?

Who do you want to be that is different from the people around you?

Being different is your superpower.

Now I lead a thriving global movement because being different forced me to create my own unique method and *make it my thing.*

Embodiment Queens across the globe sign into the *Body Talk Membership* every day and do the somatic practices. I created something different.

You're different because you're pioneering something that has never been done before

Not fitting in and having a different perspective doesn't mean you don't belong, it means you are the one who gets to create the space for other people like you to belong.

Anyone can be a coach, but you are not anyone.

You have a unique method that is so different that you don't see it anywhere else, because the person pioneering the path is YOU.

Excuses

It was my first official snow day.

Growing up in Australia, I had gone skiing once or twice and visited the United States when there was slushy gray snow on the sidewalk, but this was my first time living in a place that had a real winter.

I opened my eyes, and the first thing I saw in the morning was the most beautiful sight — a thick blanket of white snow covering the whole street. We had just moved into our first place together, a rustic Airbnb with a small room in a shared house.

I woke Kfir up with so much excitement and begged him to come out to the snow with me.

He looked at me as if I was crazy.

This was his third winter in Boston and he said it would be so much more fun to stay snuggled under the warm covers on our day off than go on an adventure and enjoy the most beautiful snow day outside.

Your nervous system will always make excuses to choose the warm, fuzzy comfort blanket rather than stepping outside in a blizzard of discomfort.

In that moment, all the body was focused on was staying away from the discomfort of the cold, even though the conscious mind knew how much more enjoyable it would be to go and make memories in the snow.

The choice became the short-term fun of staying comfortable and warm or the long-term enjoyment from short-term discomfort.

Don't use 'listening to your body' as an excuse to stay small or slow down.

Don't confuse alignment with

waiting for all the steps to be clear.

Don't confuse grounding with

waiting for it to be easy.

Don't confuse the right time

with feeling relaxed in your body.

Don't confuse growth with

comfort.

The nervous system will always choose familiar suffering over unfamiliar success.

Nervous system expansion is about making choices and taking action with fear rather than letting the nervous system make the decisions for you.

Growth doesn't actually feel fun, easeful, or enjoyable in your body.

The journey to receiving with ease happens through the period of uncomfortable stretching.

Deserving

You don't deserve to have your offers fill up with the most embodied women just because you're an incredible coach.

You earn an overflowing business that feels grounded in your nervous system by devoting yourself to your audience.

You don't have the right words yet because you're not having a conversation.

The articulation, clarity, and expression come via the act of SPEAKING!

Embodiment Queens are the best at making money because they are so deeply connected to the language of the body.

My client, who is a powerful embodiment coach, just doubled her income in a week!

We didn't do any sessions about content or selling. All we did was embodiment and somatic shifts of beliefs in the body.

My client is such an incredible coach and was trying to articulate the power of her work on social media but felt there was a gap in reaching the women she knew she could deeply serve.

She was posting content and promoting her offers, but nothing changed until we made this one shift...

EMBODIED PROMOTION

People invest in feelings.

Not just information.

Your superpower lies in your ability to make your audience FEEL.

She turned her promotion from a feeling like a to-do list, to a soulful emotional human-to-human connection.

Imagine two dancers:

- The first hits all the right choreography steps, receives applause, goes home, and repeats the routine the next day.

- Now, picture Dancer 2, who has the audience on their toes from the moment she enters the stage. Eyes full of tears, season passes bought during intermission, and a roaring standing ovation follow.

Key difference?

Emotion

It's not just about movement.

It's about moving people.

The same goes for making money.

It's not about hitting the right steps, and doing all the things perfectly from the marketing gurus...

It's your capacity to make someone FEEL something.

You are an Embodiment Queen if you were dancing before you could walk.

You shine in the spotlight just as brightly as you do in your bedroom in PJs.

Dance is your devotion. Movement is your prayer.

The language of emotion is your mother tongue.

Your body tells a story, and in the act of dancing, you give permission for people to FEEL so alive.

What truly sets you apart when it comes to making money is your profound capacity to make someone FEEL.

You know it's not just about hitting the right steps; it's about speaking the language your audience truly understands: <u>emotion</u>.

Your clients love working with you for a reason.

The referrals and word-of-mouth clients pouring in are a testament to your emotional attunement to their needs.

They FEEL something special in your sessions.

All we get to do is transfer this powerful skill you already have into your promotion.

Falling

You don't find your superpower; you fall into it, and your capacity to rise through it is where it becomes yours.

You are so embodied in your medicine because you intimately know the pain of not having it.

Your capacity to give those tools to yourself is your capacity to share your gift with the world.

But a part of you feels like you can't hold it all.

A deeper calling has a deeper falling.

Your courage to come face-to-face with the unworthiness of this fall, expands your capacity to hold so much more attention, visibility, impact, and responsibilities.

This happens when you speak your message even louder, and sell your offers with even more pride in the times where you have fallen.

When you fall even deeper, your capacity to hold yourself and your journey back up each time will strengthen your muscle of holding more.

When you take your body through the depth of worthiness,

liberate the core of the pain body,

the blocked emotions,

and the beliefs that live there.

You're able to call forth the most worthy and wealthy version of yourself.

Responsibility

Your nervous system doesn't know the difference between joy from making less money and having fewer responsibilities, and the joy that comes from recurring income that brings more options and more responsibilities.

You don't need to work harder.

Look at all the hard-working employees — they work way harder than the manager, but the manager gets paid <u>more</u>.

Why?

Because the manager holds more responsibility and leadership in their nervous system.

Good news: You don't need to climb any corporate ladders to do this.

Only the ladder of your nervous system capacity.

The difference is the Worker Bee vs Queen Bee.

The Queen doesn't do it all.

She focuses on creation and lets her community, her

creations, do the work for her.

Your job isn't to work the hardest.

It's to let what you create do the work for you.

It's time to transition from Worker Bee to Queen Bee.

This doesn't mean lifting your hands and surrendering. This means getting even more focused on your time and your actions, doubling down on your zone of genius, and generously pouring value into your community.

This means stopping the busy work of perfecting sales pages, and websites, or searching for trending audios.

Here's how:

1.   Bring your knowledge into your body.

What happens often is you practice all the knowledge in the mind, then get overwhelmed by the details and skip the step of internalizing it in the body.

Logic and understanding are great, but if the body doesn't catch up to the mind, it turns into overwhelm instead of integration.

Bringing all this incredible wisdom you have into the body can be as simple as starting the day with a five-minute embodiment practice.

2.   Own your doubt.

It's common to try to skip past doubt, to fix it, or to try to release it and get rid of it.

This actually creates an even bigger gap and separation between your clients and audience.

Instead, connect to the discomfort of doubting yourself.

What's the underlying pain?

Why is this so important to you?

What's even deeper than that?

Feel that discomfort in your body and give your powerful tools to yourself.

3. Be the embodiment of what you teach.

Be the embodiment by taking that pain you felt in Step 2 and witnessing it, feeling it, accepting it, and practicing non-resistance by facing it head-on.

What is it really saying?

What is it asking for?

Go do that thing, and then use this pain as fuel to do something about it!

This is the exact opportunity to be the embodiment of what you teach.

4. Create balance for your masculine.

The biggest mistake for many embodiment coaches is getting stuck in 'masculine' steps in my business — the website, Zoom, payments, etc.

People aren't signing up with your website, they're signing up because they FEEL something when you talk, when you move, when you share your voice, when you invite them to workshops and challenges.

Go make sure you are sharing your voice more than doing the busy work that doesn't actually serve your audience.

5. Shift beliefs in your body.

Not fully embodied.

Lack of focus.

Being all over the place.

These are beliefs, not truths.

They hold man-made conditioning, that you have to be perfect to be a coach, that you have to be focused on being successful, and that all over the place is a bad thing.

When we get to the root of these beliefs in the body, we hear the deeper request, your deeper truth.

6. Your Superpower

Your superpower and what makes you unique is exactly what takes you outside the box, not what keeps you following all the rules of what every other coach on the internet is doing.

This is the power to view every 'limitation' as proof you are winning and every 'struggle' as an opportunity to transform it into your super-power!

Quantum Leap

It's my 30th birthday, and I feel like my life is over.

I am in a doorless helicopter riding over the most iconic mountains and ocean of Kauai, but all I want to do is throw myself out just so I could end the intense, painful nausea I was experiencing.

The winds were strong, the turbulence was super rough, and I don't know if I was shaking from the vibration of the powerful engine or from my body being in such shock.

Everyone wants to quantum leap, but no one wants the altitude sickness that comes with rapid speed.

I was so excited to do the famous helicopter ride over the most incredible view in the entire world on my 30th birthday.

I worked so hard to get there, but in the actual experience, my body could not handle it. I got so nauseous and spent the second half of the flight with my eyes closed, praying for it to be over.

Your business quantum leap is only as powerful as your nervous system can hold rapid speed and shocking change. Those words themselves are considered textbook trauma, but it's also the exact somatic experience of a quantum leap.

Massive growth experiences turbulence in the body with intense panic, freeze, worry, and nausea.

It really is not for everyone.

Many coaches stay comfortable with an income level for long periods because the nervous system refuses to undergo the quantum crumble.

But trailblazers, pioneers, and changemakers use that discomfort as fuel to impact thousands with their unique method.

It's time to reframe shock into massive growth, and train your body with the capacity to be able to hold a quantum leap.

Your social media is blowing up, your clients are getting the most incredible transformations, and you're invested in more than one business mastermind. Yet, your nervous system is still in freeze mode.

You can work so hard for a milestone. You envision it. It looks so great from the outside. And then when it's here, the body is a whole different story.

This is exactly why the nervous system capacity to hold massive amounts of wealth is more important than just being able to receive it.

Great heights take great amounts of capacity.

Grit

It's 6am, and most of the quiet beach town in Panama is fast asleep, aside from a couple of surfers eager to catch the sunrise riding the waves.

I put on my pink ribbed bathing suit and carry a longboard double my height to get washed around in the ocean and greet the beautiful day ahead.

I sat on the board, watching the sun start to peak over the sleepy town, and said a little prayer.

Please God, give me the courage and clarity to start my own successful online business.

With all the uncertainty of not knowing where my income would come from and not having a way to get back home because flights had all been canceled, my constant was the ocean.

I was not a talented surfer, and it took me weeks to get the hang of it, but what I did have was devotion.

This skill, this grit, this commitment back then is the same muscle that allowed me to build a global movement that four years later, while riding an epic wave in Hawaii, I made $30k from my online business.

You don't need the full picture, but what you do need is the courage to commit.

I couldn't have even dreamed this would be my life four years later — writing a book and being known for creating a unique somatic success method but much like surfing, it's less about riding the wave, and more about your devotion to getting back out there, wave after wave.

Shame

"You did WHAT?" I thought my eyes would pop out of my head.

How did my client casually just drop that her work supported a woman who had gone from experiencing blindness to restoring a level of eyesight in just a few sessions with her?

I was shocked but not surprised.

I have the most insanely gifted, talented, wise, powerful clients, and every time, I am blown away by what they do versus how they present what they do online.

The first thing I have my clients do is list their achievements and accomplishments, and it's often the most challenging thing for them to do.

No matter how powerful your work is, if shame is ruling the show, it's going to make it very difficult for your clients to want to pay you, and even if they are ready, it will make it hard for you to receive that money.

Shame is beyond logic.

It's a real feeling based on conditioning and belief systems that live in your body.

The truth is, shame never goes away; it transforms into power when witnessed.

Within the first two weeks of liberating shame from her body, this client had made $10k, then went on to have $20k months and, a couple of months later, $45k month as a healer and mom of five.

Here are the steps we explored to transform shame into her superpower:

1.   Shame is a portal to deep service.

You were given gifts for a reason.

Repressed shame in the body makes you think it's all about you.

When you take a deeper look, you realize your gifts are gifts.

Your medicine is divine.

It's bigger than you.

You are the messenger.

Your gifts were gifted to YOU so you can facilitate them to others.

Conditioning will have you believe this is bragging, but when you zoom out, you will realize this is what devotion and service actually look like.

When you allow your promotion to be about what becomes possible for your client, you embrace the role of being a messenger.

You acknowledge that you're sharing your client's transformations, which were given not for personal glorification but as a means to facilitate healing for others.

2.   Shame is a portal to powerful leadership.

Real humility is leadership, the type that owns your skills and takes others along with you.

Keeping your wins quiet is taking away the opportunity from someone else to have that experience.

Ego pride makes it about you.

What will others think of me when I share how powerful my work is?

Ouch, that will make me vulnerable to judgment.

Divine pride makes it about service.

You care more about the impact of sharing how powerful your work is over what others will think or say about you.

3.   Shame is a portal to empowerment.

Shame is asking you to remember what your soul is here for.

When you tell your story, when you share your personal transformations, it's more than just getting something off your chest to feel better.

It becomes a seed of possibility for others.

Your story is a pathway for someone to believe it's possible for them.

Are you ready to integrate and embody this?

- Boast about your powerful work on your social media today.

- What have you achieved for yourself?

- What have your clients achieved through your work?

- What makes your work so special and unique?

  Notice the discomfort in your body as you share, and remember that, in this exact action, you are liberating deep-conditioned shame and transforming it into service, leadership, and empowerment!

Courage

Some of you need a little less spirituality and a little more courage to sell your face off.

There is a societal belief that medicine work shouldn't charge a lot, that helping people should be free, or that wealth is dangerous, unsafe, or greedy, etc.

What this belief system is actually saying is that your time is not valuable.

Money doesn't buy happiness, but it does buy you the financial capacity to pour generously into the organizations you care so deeply about and most importantly, pour into your most important asset — your time.

The more you value your time, your skills, your gifts, and your medicine, the more change you get to create in the world.

Even though your mind may logically know this, your body often holds onto conditioning and passed down beliefs.

In order to liberate this belief from your nervous system and train your body to feel worthy of your time, value your skills and your medicine. You need to liberate disgust around money in your body.

Disgust releases beliefs from the body in the form of a physical purge; sometimes, this practice will have you spitting or coughing.

What happens is that you tangibly throw up these beliefs that are no longer serving you from your system.

In order to integrate this practice, after this practice, go out and sell your offers with conviction in your body. It will feel edgy and uncomfortable and it's supposed to.

When you lean into this edge and take bold action, you move from valuing your time internally to actually embodying that in the action.

Your gifts are too important for them to be hidden behind resistance, fear, excuses, and discomfort.

Anyone can claim they want to heal the world and create liberation for all of humanity, but the women who are actually creating global impact are the ones helping more people.

You don't need more out-of-body spiritual practices and another cacao ceremony for peace and love. You need the courage it takes to serve more people. And that happens when you get your offers into the hands of more people by selling them.

Your income isn't just the numbers in your bank account; it's a reflection of the number of lives you impact.

Don't confuse being an *influencer* with being of *influence*.

An influencer has thousands of followers.

Being of influence has thousands of testimonials AND makes hundreds of thousands of dollars while being of deep service.

The most powerful embodiment coaches are not the ones with the most followers. They are the ones with the most impact.

Here's how:

1. Raise Your Boundaries

Level 1 of your embodied product suite is your free and low ticket offers.

What's holding you back from having so much time and wealth is that you allow people to have access to your time at this level. Spending hours in your DMs answering questions and responding with lengthy replies to comments is not leadership. It's friend-zoning the clients ready to pay you thousands for your high-level mentorship.

Level 1 of your embodied product suite is 1:many, which means it takes you the same amount of time and has unlimited capacity for people it can impact. Some examples are Instagram Lives, memberships, workshops, or offers under $100. To scale your Level 1 to hundreds of members and recurring monthly income, you must raise your boundaries so that your time is making more impact.

2. Raise Your Standards

Level 2 of your embodied product suite is your mid-ticket offers or group programs.

What's holding you back from filling up your groups with many clients is unclear or savior messaging and sneaky somatic martyrdom in your coaching. This looks like obsessing over your clients' results, trying to hold them rather than guide them, or saying they are doing amazing when really they would thrive with direct leadership.

Level 2 of your product suite has a little more access to you, and the focus here gets to be on how the group can guide each other using your method so that you do not need to answer everyone, but you have created a dynamic that is still so deeply supportive and transformation. This level can hold many clients without adding more calls to your calendar or getting on sales calls.

3. Raise Your Prices

Level 3 of your embodied product suite is your high ticket 1:1, or mastermind offers

What's holding you back from having the clients that you want is the value of your time, aka your pricing. People pay more for luxury, rapid, and personalized transformation.

You are charging a fraction of what your transformation creates for your clients' lives because you carry beliefs that because your work is spiritual, it should be free or at least affordable. The message this actually reinforces is that spirituality is martyrdom, and you should sacrifice your life and your desires for everyone other than yourself.

Level 3 of your product suite is your highest asset, your time, and access to you. This is where it's actually time to raise your prices and only work with people who fill you with so much life-force energy. This level creates a large percentage of your recurring income from the least amount of people. 80% of your income comes from 20% of your clients, so when you create the most incredible luxury experiences for these clients, you actually get so much time and income.

Greed

O kay, I can't believe I'm about to admit this, but I am greedy.

I post on social media, and I always want more followers and likes.

I make more in a month than some in a year, and all that I can think of is, how can I get more?

The truth is, there is a purpose to greed.

When it is unprocessed, it turns into disgust, and when it's liberated, it turns into generosity.

It's easy to desire to give so much charity and want to spoil your parents, but greed and generosity live on the same emotional spectrum in your body.

If you suppress greed, you are suppressing generosity.

I know it sounds backwards, but the desire for more is neutral.

Only when you judge it, does it feel bad for having its desires, so it hides it.

When something is pushed down long enough, it rears its head in more ugly ways.

When I was in high school, there were no unhealthy snacks in my house, and every time I went to my friend's house, I would stuff my face in her pantry, which was full of chocolates, snack bars, and candy.

The candy in this story is completely neutral. When it's hidden in my house for being 'bad,' the need for it comes out in even more unhealthy ways.

It is the same with the desire for more, complete neutrality.

When it's judged for being wrong or disgusting, we self-sabotage our own desires through procrastination, comparisons, and distraction.

When processed, cleared, and liberated from the body, greed can become a tool of so much giving.

We can only be truly generous when we stop demonizing greed and start celebrating the human desire for more.

Today, I invite you to celebrate your greed, make space for it in your body, and to move through your system.

I assure you, when you listen to what it has to say, you will actually have the capacity to be so much more generous.

The difference between a successful coaching business and a global movement is the capacity for MORE in your body.

So you reached the milestones in your business that you worked so hard for, and you realize that being booked out was never the goal!

Well, congratulations, you are not alone!

This is a massive collective shift that is happening in the space of changemakers!

You are feeling the tug because you know deep down, you're meant for MORE...

There are two types of MORE:

- MORE in your coaching business: There is more strategy, more posting, more clients, more work, more sacrifice, more milestones to reach, and more tasks to tick off the never-ending to-do list... you get the gist.

- MORE in your global movement: There is more capacity, more energy, more impact, more ripple effect of change in the world.

Picture this:

You're so busy working, but your hunger gets too loud, so you finally open the fridge, find some leftovers, and quickly scarf them down on the couch.

You finish your bowl, and your stomach makes a small growl.

You feel full, but there is this sensation and feeling of wanting more.

Now picture this:

It's Friday night, the candles are lit, and your living room is filled with all your favorite people.

There is a gorgeous flower arrangement on the table that your husband brought home alongside the beautifully set table.

Your home is filled with the delicious smell of the coming dinner, laughter, and singing.

You get this little grumbling sensation in your stomach, and you feel so excited about so much more of this.

MORE in the body can come from lack.

Or MORE can come from the sense of overflow.

Your nervous system doesn't actually know the difference between these two desires for more, because they have very similar physical sensations and feelings in the body.

Many coaches remain in this tiring chase of more milestones.

What they really want is more impact, more peace, more presence.

This is because your body doesn't know the difference between these two types of MORE.

Belief #1 is more greed.

And Belief #2 is more generosity.

So, how do you make this and shift your core belief systems in your body?

Step 1:

- Become aware of how your body is driven by more.

- For example, anxious energy from all the things you want to accomplish in the day.

Step 2:

- Somatically shift the core belief around more in your body, from more greed to more generosity.

- (No amount of mindset or self-awareness will shift beliefs in your body.)

Step 3:

- Action: Take this anxious energy and decide to create, overdeliver, serve, and transform this electric current of moving energy into magnetic selling that has your clients become walking testimonials for you.

Capacity

Being regulated and relaxed is not going to help you double your income.

The word safety does not exist in my containers because radical growth and having hundreds of people join your offers does not feel "safe, cozy, or comfortable" in your body.

A lot of the time, it feels daunting, terrifying, embarrassing, and overwhelming because it's not about feeling good; it's about getting really good at feeling.

You're only limited by that which you don't allow yourself to feel. The deeper grief you can feel, the more capacity you have to sell with conviction because you choose to care more about your clients' results than the fear of annoying people.

The deeper disappointment you can feel, the more capacity you have to do something with that frustration and shake up the world with the fiery offers you know will change thousands of lives.

Selling isn't about avoiding rejection; it's about prioritizing your clients' transformations over your own fears.

You can have all the nervous system trainings in the world, but if your body panics or freezes when you are upleveling, it's not a sign to calm down your nervous system.

It's a cry for the fire within to turn into brave expression, taking up even more space and selling bigger than ever.

You don't need more nervous system regulation; you need more capacity, because the fear never goes away. Your capacity to take action with fear gets stronger.

When you understand that your income is a mirror of your nervous system, you realize it's less about how much you do and more about your capacity to hold it all.

Anyone can be a coach.

Anyone can post on social media.

But you're not anyone.

You're the person who transforms discomfort into pioneering a new path.

You're the person who can hold an unlimited capacity of members because of how unapologetic you are with selling and promoting your unique membership.

You're the person who doesn't just build a coaching business, but develops a unique method that impacts thousands.

You're the person who owns your voice and creates your own unique way of self-expression.

Stretching your nervous system capacity doesn't happen by learning about the nervous system behind closed doors, in a journal entry, a somatic practice, or even a breathwork session.

It happens in the uncomfortable action you continuously take after that experience that actually stretches your nervous system capacity.

How could you stretch this month?

How could you over-deliver?

How could you commit to an even higher level of service?

What would it look like to practically devote even deeper into your content and clients?

Generosity

I forget how to breathe for a moment.

My eyes widen, and I have goosebumps on my arms.

"A hundred and eighty dollars," this person said in the most gentle, casual way.

I have been sitting by the phone the whole day.

It's a telethon — a day of fundraising to raise money for the Jewish Community Center my family ran.

I really dislike asking people for money.

I'm already 12 years old, and I recognize some of the family names on printed-out pieces of paper I was assigned to call.

What if my friends answer the phone? What if my friends knew I was spending my Sunday calling hundreds of people, asking them to help us keep our center afloat?

I don't have many friends as it is.

I wish I were one of the cool, popular girls, who could read magazines, go shopping, and actually buy new clothes.

"Do you want my credit card details?"

I am back in reality — yes, I feel like I won the lottery!

I carefully take down number after number — my hand shaking with excitement and nerves.

My father will be so proud of me. He works day and night for the community, and this will help him continue to be able to give.

I am about to hang up the call with this woman, but I long to hear her voice and grab onto any pieces of her. She feels so powerful to me. A woman, able to give so much — I want to be like her one day.

I say thank you for perhaps the tenth time before I can't stall any longer, and I let the lady hang up. I stay for a few extra minutes with the phone next to my ear. I don't want this moment to end.

It felt so easy — is this what generosity feels like?

Then why am I on this side of the phone calling this God's work?

If both sides are divine, I want to be on the other side of the line.

I look around the room, and my brothers and sisters and some helpers are making calls, ticking names off lists, and calling and asking for donations.

I close my eyes.

I promise myself one day, I am going to be on the other side of the line.

***

I just got off the phone with my niece.

She was so excited to tell me she won a camera you could print as a prize for receiving a big donation I had made in her name.

Today, I get to be on the other side of the line.

Belief System Practice

Your beliefs rule your business, not your brain.

Your capacity to listen to what those beliefs are saying in your body and do something about them is what will set you free.

It can get frustrating to make affirmations and set intentions and journal, but your being is still holding on so tightly to an old belief.

Understanding the old beliefs is great, but most people miss the most important part: integrating that belief in your body.

Here are the three steps to shift on a body level:

- **1. Proof:** The first step is to become open to the possibility of believing this new belief one day. Find examples proving this belief to be true, collect the evidence, and make it clear to your nervous system that this is a possibility. Say yes to the belief. Play with the belief.

- **2. Practice:** Create space and time to play with the belief. How much time would you give yourself to work on this belief? If you fully embody them, how would they change your life and business? Walk like you have this belief, talk like it, take up space, move as if this is already your belief, and integrate that into your life, conversations, content, and most importantly, take action from this version of you that fully lives this belief.

- **3. Drama:** The universe will ask you if you really want this belief, more than once or twice. It isn't a simple copy-and-paste process. The test phase strengthens your own trust in this belief. Use these opportunities as signs that you are embodying and processing — as proof that this new belief is really working.

Are you ready to experience this incredible chapter in your body?

You can do this somatic practice for each belief or emotion around receiving wealth and money in your nervous system.

1. Begin by filling out the desire that you are calling in.

2. What is the block, belief, or emotion getting in the way?

3. Go into the body, breath, sensation, posture, and movement. Notice how that block is serving you and the core desire it has underneath.

4. How can you give yourself this same core desire in a new shape, posture, and movement in your body?

5. Determine these two belief systems both = the core desire.

6. Write down what actions live on the old belief and in the new belief and use the fuel of this block to channel into taking the action that creates the reality of the new belief.

7. Keep this as your unique success code.

Desire	
Block	Building block
How is this block actually serving you? What does this character receive in this state? What is the Core Desire here?	
Old Belief Block_____= Core Desire _____	New Belief New possibility _____= Core desire_____
Body/sensation/emotions/shape	Body/sensation/emotions/shape
Actions/Habits	Actions/Habits

Acknowledgments

I never realized how privileged I was to grow up in a Hasidic Jewish home until I entered the self-development world and realized everything I was hearing was so familiar.

The teachings in this book are all accredited to the wisdom of Kabbalah, Jewish mystical teachings that experience Godliness in our 3D world, our bodies.

I would like to dedicate this book to my teachers.

To my parents for being the biggest role models of what connection to God looks like and modeling to me how to make this world a brighter place by being so generous and giving to the family and to our community.

To my grandparents, ancestors, and Jewish lineage, thank you for the privilege of standing on your shoulders of sacrifice, connection, and tradition that allows me to carry such pride in my roots so I can continue growing this beautiful tree of life.

To Kfir, thank you for believing in my vision, for the patience in becoming this version of me, and for picking me up on the days that feel like it's all too heavy.

To my somatic teacher, Maya Night, eternal gratitude for teaching me skills that have completely transformed my life, my income, and the legacy I get to create.

To my business coaches, Bridget James Ling and Shoshanah Raven, thank you for being the proof of what's possible for me in the most fun, feminine, powerful, and alive way.

To my clients, I'm humbled that you chose me to guide and facilitate you on your powerful journey.

To my dear reader, thank you for taking the time to explore this powerful work and for making me an author!

Connect with Sheina:

The book doesn't end here. This is just the beginning of a powerful journey of continuously encoding wealth in your body.

Instagram: I love connecting to you here. My DMs are open, and you can tag me when you share a picture of yourself reading the *Body Talk* book! I am excited to hear your biggest takeaways and personal transformations! You can find me @sheinaraskin

Podcast: Listen to the *Body Talk Show* by Sheina Raskin while you're on a road trip, on your morning walk, or in the background while you play with your kids. These episodes will infuse your body with so much energy, drive, and excitement to create, express, share, and sell in a way that feels so alive for you. Search *Body Talk Show* on Spotify and Apple Podcasts.

EMBODIMENT INDEX

There is no such thing as blocks, only building blocks.

This book isn't a one-time read. It's a powerful manual that is unique to your body.

This index is here to quickly reference a sensation you desire to feel or shift in your body.

Hundreds of Embodiment Queens are ready to welcome you inside our online membership and community, Body Talk, to deepen this experience and encode next-level wealth and impact in your body.

Click here to join and use the code: book for the $22 special invitation.

https://sheina.kartra.com/page/membership

ABUNDANCE OF SALES

You get to thrive in business when your body is in the state of thriving. The most underrated success strategy is preparing your nervous system to receive the dream clients and opportunities.

There's ready on paper, and then there's ready in your BODY! Set yourself up to thrive by inviting in the sensation of thriving and notice what comes up for you. Where is there resistance? What does thriving mean to you? Let yourself feel the sensation of thriving in the body FIRST, and then take action from this space.

CONFIDENCE

What you see is someone posting with confidence, and what you don't see is the embodiment that allows them to transform their shame into powerful storytelling. What you see is someone selling with pride, and what you don't see is the embodiment that allows them to transform their money blocks into a deeper sense of self-trust. The reality is that your clients want to buy from you BECAUSE of all the pieces that make YOU unique. You're worried the truth will scare them away, but what is actually scaring them away is you not accepting all parts of yourself first. Begin to invite in the sensation of being PROUD of yourself for your experience and accomplishments. Practicing this feeling of pride regularly anchors your nervous system into confidence.

CONFUSION AND CLARITY

Your capacity for confusion is your capacity to pioneer a new way. Confusion and clarity are two ends of the same spectrum. Your clarity comes when you take action despite the confusion. Your ability to sit with the confusion and take action anyway is your capacity to trailblaze a new path that brings you the clarity you seek. Stop looking for clarity. Look for courage. The courage to be different is pioneering. There isn't clarity because it hasn't been done before. YOU'RE THE ONE TO DO IT! Go do that thing right now!

CONSISTENCY

If consistency feels like pressure or rules that you have to follow, here is a reframe for you. You get to do consistency in YOUR way! Instead of having to be consistent for the algorithm, you get to be consistently inspired, consistently in a state of art, and consistently have poetry come out of your lips. You get to be consistently turned on, consistently in your state. Own consistency when you CREATE it from within your body as opposed to rules to follow outside of you.

CONTROL

Control is a muscle for trust in God. Let God do God's work, which is the end result. Let your soul do your soul's work, which is creating the container and vessel to be able to receive the result. What does creating this vessel in action look like for you today?

CULTIVATING COMMUNITY AND CELEBRATION

The best shift for your body to believe it's possible is to get around other bodies that believe it's possible! Self-celebration, and sharing your wins and accomplishments expands your nervous system to be able to receive so much more! Today I'm celebrating three years of business, of courage, of devotion, of embodiment, and sharing with you the body codes of how to experience grounded success with joy and ease in your body! What are you celebrating today?

DISTRACTION

Distraction is running away from an uncomfortable feeling. There is nothing to say to make you want to change the distraction, so don't say anything, don't fix anything. Just be here with the distraction without any goal or intention. Just be with it.

DIVINE TIMING

Your mind saying you're ready is very different from your body saying you're ready. Divine timing happens not when your mind chooses it's convenient, but when your body actually is open and allowing for this thing to happen. Try movement practices that open your heart, your hips, your eyes, your jaws, and your hands, and prepare your body for so much success, joy, responsibility, and wealth

EROTIC MAGNETISM

As women, we literally have days in the month where we're a chemically attracting and powerful magnetic force! This is more powerful than any strategy or any copy! Your ovulation period is a great time to schedule photoshoots or to film yourself! You don't have to be ON every day, but when you are, capture it!!

FLOW STATE

Getting into the flow state is the most underrated, yet simple practice that you can do daily that makes success inevitable. This gets your mind and body into the frequency of focus, flow, and activation. This is the quickest way to shift beliefs, clear blocks, and expand your nervous system capacity to receive more money! Get into the flow state by embodying YOU and staying in your lane. Where is your soul calling you right now?

GIVE UP

Feeling like you want to give up is an opportunity for a death and rebirth cycle. What about this really does need giving up? What part needs letting go? Our feelings and emotions are maps to our success.

Learn how to listen. Maybe it's a past version of you that needs to die; maybe a belief system is asking to be liberated. These moments are opportunities for real transformation. If you can get through this, you can build your nervous system to handle the next level of growth. Remember, growth feels damn uncomfortable, often like a death. Your capacity to experience this discomfort and pain in your body is your capacity to invite in so much clarity, joy, and ease into your body.

GROWTH

Growth is your capacity to grieve. Growing pains are real. You have to become someone else in order to step into who you want to become. It's painful to let go of your past self and often involves an emotional death. This is stretching and expanding what your nervous system is used to receiving, so it has space for so much more. Let yourself grieve today. Do a somatic practice where you honor your past aspects (maybe invite in pictures, old relics, etc.) and then thank them for their role/wisdom.

HEARTBREAK OR AN ACHING HEART

Fragile does not mean weak. Easily triggered and emotional does not make you weak. Your heart may feel delicate, but that is what makes it precious, so treat it gently and with extra care. Slow down, nourish your body with a warm, homey meal, or tuck yourself into bed earlier. Dance. Move. This dance is dedicated to heartbreak. Tend to your broken heart and allow it to be fuel to add more empathy, love, respect, and light into the world by first embodying that with yourself. Your sadness and grief is a powerful tool for stability and support. Let it move through you, and let yourself sit with it without needing to do anything. Both of these practices will transform your relationship with your aching heart.

HOPE

Tragedy is too much for the mind to fathom. So we have to go deeper than the mind and into the body. To play in the realm of hope, we have to first create space in the body to believe that a positive outcome is possible. For many, despair is the natural pattern the body will gravitate towards and this is why it's so important to guide the body into a new pattern of hope. When you are feeling despair, learn to look for what is being birthed through this despair. Where are you being led? What are you being led into? What new experiences are now possible?

JUDGMENT + CARING ABOUT NUMBERS OR METRICS

Judgment isn't bad, as long as you give it proportion. For every time you check how many likes you got, you get to channel that judgment into celebrating every individual human being that took the time to watch your content. There probably wouldn't be enough time in the day and then your body gets to realize how to actually move through that judgment of caring about numbers into caring about the numbers as actual people. Judgment is caring, so ask yourself how do you want to channel this human feeling of caring?

LEVELING UP

Somatic practices for upleveling up include getting your body into the state of what you are creating. This chapter is about to be massive. Get your body ready to carry and receive all of it! How can you expand your capacity today? What can you do that stretches your edges? Think physically, mentally, emotionally, and spiritually.

MAGNETISM

Being seen is a primal desire. Embrace your natural seductress, your inner flirt with life. The feminine energy, by nature, is alluring and magnetic, not by doing or achieving, but by simply claiming your love for attention and accepting your own liberated self before accepting others to do so.

NEEDING TO KNOW

Certainty is a primal core desire and it can turn into fear and overwhelm when repressed. But how? Your body is craving answers. On a deeper level, what is it really asking you? What is the sensation of knowing? It might be asking for softness, for permission to enjoy the way; perhaps it's asking for you to make a decision so it knows which direction it can move towards.

NERVES

I like to imagine nervous energy as being star-struck. They are so excited by this powerful light that they are frozen and don't know what to do with themselves. When they realize that they themselves ARE THE STAR, the nerves get to transform into excitement and confidence.

NUMBNESS

It can happen that, at times, our body feels safer to not feel than to feel anything. Notice the desire underneath the numbness. What feeling is the numbness protecting you from, and can you give yourself a moment to experience this discomfort?

OVERTHINKING

You don't find your voice by thinking or contemplating. You find it through talking, creating, posting, expressing, and giving a voice to all the incredible ideas you have in your mind. Channel that overthinking into creative expression today.

OVERWORKING

Being so busy can be a distraction from a repressed emotion that's uncomfortable to feel. When you get to move it through your system, the busy energy gets to be transformed into powerful boundaries and self-trust. The tighter you hold on, the less you can hold!

PEOPLE PLEASING

There's nothing wrong with pleasing people; it's just a matter of WHO you are pleasing. If people pleasing comes naturally to you — congratulations — you're a stand-out changemaker. You care about other people and making an impact! Now, you get to channel all this energy into caring MORE about the impact, more than the opinions, needs, and desires of others.

PURPOSE

Darkness is when the body is feeling heavy, overwhelmed, and hearing loud voices of self-pity and uncertainty. To liberate this energy is to choose to channel this energy for light, for drive, responsibility, focus, and generosity. It might seem like the body is just asking for sleep and to give up; it takes courage to do the exact opposite and get into an energetic state of excitement and passion to do something that feels meaningful.

REMEMBER YOUR POWER

You see the falling. Everyone else sees your courage to get back up. Powerful doesn't mean you never fall; it means you never let the fall define you.

RESISTANCE

Dancing

WITH tension

WITH anxious energy

WITH fear

WITH shame

Is the pathway for liberation.

Invite it in.

SCARCITY

The frequency of scarcity is going to make you so wealthy. Scarcity is what is so rare, so precious. Time is something that is scarce that you don't have a lot of. Treat time with scarcity as a rare precious jewel. Scarcity is not something to get rid of; it's something to channel. Let it funnel into the things that actually are scarce. You need both the capacity to feel scarcity and abundance to be able to receive so much of the thing that you are calling in.

SELF-ACCEPTANCE

Deep levels of accepting yourself don't happen in a meditation or a journaling practice. It happens in the action of taking up space, pressing record, listening to your voice, and the capacity to choose to fully accept that exact version of you. Embodiment is the action you take.

SELF-TRUST

When you find yourself searching for inspiration for the type of life you want to live, your body is actually asking you for permission to validate yourself at this moment. Searching for answers from people you look up to and a sense of uncertainty within is a sign that it's time to choose yourself, celebrate your uniqueness, and share your story with the world. No one is out there like you — this is your time to turn up the dial of YOU!

SENSUAL CREATION + SELF-EXPRESSION

Touch is a powerful expander for self-expression and content creation through pleasure and sensual delight. Your capacity to touch yourself and enjoy the love language of touch is the capacity to touch someone with your words, art, and content. Touch is a core love language of connecting to your audience, and it starts with you inviting touch in your movement practice.

SOULFUL CONTENT

You can't do it all, but... You can have the capacity to receive it all. This is the difference between the Worker Bee versus the Queen Bee. The Queen doesn't do it all. She has support, and she focuses on creation. Your job isn't to work the hardest; it's to let what you create do the work for you. When you create embodied content, you go from Worker Bee to Queen Bee.

STUCK SCROLLING

Scrolling helps the body to not feel sadness. Build the courage to pause a moment, close your eyes, and hug yourself. Breathe into your chest and exhale into your belly to create some space for emotions to flow through your body. Create space to cry, to let the tears flow. It's unhealthy to watch the news without giving yourself space to actually feel.

TRUSTING YOUR INTUITION

Intuition is gaining information through the senses, feelings, and instincts that live in your BODY, not in your mental thinking! The practice of trusting your full body yes is following what it feels like to feel alive. Intuition is a muscle, so we need to practice watching what the body says yes to!

WAITING ZONE

The waiting zone might feel passive, but what's happening in your body is very active. Waiting is giving your power to someone or something outside of you. That same energy turns into fuel by claiming what you are creating and making the vessel for it to pour through, transforming that control from outsourced to internal.

WANTING MORE

When you want more, but your body is judging that you want more, it is an opportunity to explore deeper. Conditioning around "you should be happy with what you have," is creating guilt and disgust rather than the capacity to actually ENJOY what you have. Wanting more is actually your body asking you to enjoy what it is you DO have. What would that actually look like and feel like in your body to enjoy? Maybe slowing down, maybe celebrating, maybe deep conversations, maybe quality time? This way, when you do want more, you'll actually have the capacity in your nervous system to receive so much more!

WORRY

Trying to only have positive thoughts is great for your mind, but worry often lives in the body and can be irrational, so focusing only on thoughts doesn't necessarily release the worry. The body knows what it's doing, so practice self-trust and breathe into the worry. Notice where it lives in the body and very gently allow this worry to be experienced in your body. What does this worry want? What is it trying to ask for? This is a beautiful time to invite connection, touch, and eye-gazing, and allow the emotion behind the worry to move through your system.

Your Key Takeways and Unique Body Success Codes

Printed in Great Britain
by Amazon